The Blood

The Divine Cleansing Agent

The Blood: The Divine Cleansing Agent
By Pastor Mark Spitsbergen, ThD, MS
Copyright © 2026 by Abiding Place Ministries, San Diego, CA.

Address correspondence to:

ISBN: 979-8-9944098-7-9

Mark Spitsbergen
Abiding Place Ministries
2155 N Campo Truck Trail, Campo CA 91906
www.AbidingPlace.org
AwakeSD@me.com

All rights reserved.
Interior and Cover Layout by Graham Creative
Cover by Jake Smith

The Blood

The Divine Cleansing Agent

"You purchased us for God with Your blood from every tribe and language and people and nation, and made us kings and priests to God, and we shall reign upon the Earth."

-Revelations 5:9-10

Pastor Mark Spitsbergen, Thd, MS

Table of Contents

Introduction

"Knowing that you were not redeemed with corruptible things, such as silver and gold from your vain way of life- the traditions of your fathers, but with the precious blood of Christ, as a blameless and spotless Lamb"

1 Peter 1:18-19

Without the shedding of blood, there is no remission of sins[1]. God in His mercy determined that it would ultimately be His blood that would be offered for the sins of the whole world. Therefore, He took on the nature of sinful flesh and offered Himself as the Lamb of God who takes away the sins of the world. The life of the flesh is in the blood, and God became a man to give His blood for our spiritual life[2]. From the very beginning of the promise of a coming Redeemer, blood was shed in order to offer a sacrifice for man's redemption. The innocent had to die

---

[1] Heb 9:22

[2] Gen 9:4; Lev 17:11, 14; Mt 26:28

for the guilty. Whenever sin was committed, there had to be a ransom paid, because the wages of sin was, and is, death[3].

Many today and throughout history have failed to realize why the subject of the blood is so important to both Judaism and Christianity. As blood is fundamental to physical life, it is also fundamental to spiritual life and redemption. The blood carries within it both the breath and the healing agents of physical life. Without blood, a person cannot live, for life is in the blood. But the life-giving power of the blood extends beyond physical life, and is central also to redemption. Man had ruined His life and wrecked it with the incurable disease of sin. The only way that man could be cured and brought to life again would be through the destruction of his sin-diseased life and the recreation of a new life in God. Rather than wiping out sinful man and starting over, God brought forth a means of re-creating man: through a redemption that would transfuse the life of God into him and thereby make a new creation! Without the blood, there is no life, no forgiveness, no redemption, and no hope for mankind.

The story of the blood's role in redemption is first fully realized in the events of the Passover: when the blood served as the protective and redemptive agent for the people of Israel, on the night they were delivered from

---

[3] Num 18:22; Ezek 3:20; 18:24; Rom 6:16,23

Egypt[4]. As the Israelites were delivered from death and subsequently released from the bondage of Egypt even so everyone who trusts in the Lamb of God is set free. God became the Lamb for mankind, and offered His own blood to deliver us from death and set us free from the bondage of sin[5]. When He died on the cross, He poured out His life's blood and the tyrannical reign of sin came to an end for all who would believe. This was a spiritual release that took place when the life of God was imparted to us[6]. The blood of Jesus became the means to destroy the power of sin and wipe away the sins of the past for every individual. God's life destroyed death, and His blood cured the disease of sin. Only the blood of God can wipe away the sin of each person and consecrate their bodies as the temple of God[7].

The blood of animals was used as a representative offering of the coming Redeemer. The blood of every sacrifice – beginning with the one offered by God Himself to clothe man – spoke of what God Himself would do for us[8]. God took on the likeness of sinful flesh and became our Sin Offering[9]. Every sacrifice that was offered testified of the day that Jesus would pour out His blood on the altar of the cross. Each time a person offered the sacrifices

---

[4] Ex 12:7
[5] 1 Cor 5:7
[6] Jn 6:56; Col 1:20-22
[7] 2 Tim 1:10; 1 Cor 3:16
[8] Gen 3:21; Gal 4:4-5
[9] 2 Cor 5:21; 1 Pet 2:24

prescribed under the Law they testified of that day, knowingly or unknowingly. It was only by the blood that anyone could approach God and interact with Him. All of those sacrifices are done away with because they were all fulfilled in the final sacrifice to which they witnessed. Now each person may come into the Holy of Holies with all boldness by the blood of Jesus that has cleansed us from our sins[10].

[10] Heb. 10:19

The Sin

"Just as sin entered into the world through one man, and through sin death, so also that death has passed into all men, in that everyone sinned."

-Romans 5:12

God who alone knows the way to the abundant life that lasts forever has charged all mankind to walk in the ways of His life. God revealed His laws of life at the time that He created man in His own image and likeness. Although man was created in the image and likeness of God He would have to learn the ways of life which only God could teach. He would learn through learning obedience. God made it very clear that disobedience would result in spiritual death and ultimately in physical death. When Adam and his wife disobeyed God, they died spiritually. But God in His mercy immediately made them a promise of a coming Redeemer: the promised Seed[11]! God made the promise of the coming Redeemer and immediately

[11] Gen 3:15

offered the first sacrifice to cloth their nakedness, "...the LORD God made coats of skins for them...". Every sacrifice that took place in the Old Testament represented the ultimate sacrifice that God would make to cloth mankind once again in His inward likeness[12]. Adam did not have to forfeit his life that day for God took a representative offering and Himself poured out the blood for His sin and shame. It was God who made the first sacrifice for the sins of man and it was God who made the final sacrifice for the sins of man.

Abel, the son of Adam, offered the same sacrifice so that he could worship God. He too took the sacrifice that represented God's sacrifice when he brought the firstborn of the flock of sheep and offered it to the LORD. Abel's offering was a faith offering – a faith offering that represented the coming Redeemer, Christ Jesus[13]. It was the offering that God required and thus was referred to as a righteous offering[14]. We can properly imagine that God, who answers by fire, had respect for Abel's righteous and acceptable offering by sending His fire to consume it. To think that this was a random guess by Abel would not be in keeping with the thousands of similar sacrifices offered over the millennia to follow. All of those sacrifices would testify of what Jesus would do to redeem us with His own blood. Furthermore, the language that God used to invite

---

[12] Eph 4:24; Gal 3:16

[13] Heb 11:4; 12:24

[14] 1 Jn 3:12

Cain to also offer the appropriate sacrifice indicates that Cain also knew what God commanded. God said to Cain, "Why are you angry and sad? If you had done correctly, you would be accepted. And if you have not, then sin lies at your door." We could actually be right in saying that the "sin sacrifice" lies at your door. The Hebrew word for "sin" and "sin sacrifice" or "sin offering" are used interchangeably throughout the Old Testament. The Hebrew word for "sin sacrifice" as well as for "sin" is חַטָּאת ('chatat'). It is used a total of 293 times in the Old Testament, and of that, it is translated 117 times as "Sin Offering" and 170 times as "sin." The same principle may be understood of its usage in the New Testament when it was applied to Jesus as being "made sin" or "the sin offering"[15].

God taught Israel that the wages of sin is death, through the sacrificial offerings. Through the offering of one that was innocent on their behalf they were continually faced with their need for redemption, and of the power of the blood to supply that redemption. They would learn that without the shedding of blood, there is no forgiveness of sin[16]. They would come to understand how the blood purifies, cleanses, sanctifies, and protects those who are brought into covenant relationship by it[17]. Through the death of countless offerings, they learned that

---

[15] 2 Cor. 5:21

[16] Lev. 17:11; Heb. 9:22

[17] Lev 17:4, 14:1; Ezek 43:20, 45:18-20; Lev 16:15-16; Ex 29:20, 12:7, 13, 22

only by the blood could sin be set aside so that they could come into a relationship with a Holy God.

God would not have a relationship with men stained with sin unless there was a means of reconciliation. It was the blood which provided the needed forgiveness for sin and its deadly consequence. All the blood that poured out of those sacrifices purified the Holy things of God that had been contaminated by sin's deadly power[18]. Even when animals were slaughtered for food, careful attention to the sacredness and limitations on how the blood was to be treated had to be observed[19]. Of all things, the blood was most sacred, because it was the life of the flesh and that which God had given to make reconciliation upon His altar. Yet most of all it was so sacred because it was about the glorious mystery of Christ being manifested in the flesh to redeem man from sin with His own blood[20].

God would not dwell in the midst of sin. Therefore, God provided a means to remove its contamination. Every act of disobedience against the ways of God is sin. Sin is a capital offense against the life of God, and everyone who sinned was under a penalty of death – both then and now. Even worse sin not only contaminates the lives of the individual, but also everything that is around it[21]. Even the land that God created can not tolerate the effects of the sin

---

[18] Heb 9:22-23; Lev 16:11, 16
[19] Lev 16:13, 17:4; Isa 66:3
[20] Ac 20:28; Heb 9:12; 13:12; Rev 1:5
[21] Josh 7:24

of men because sin defiles it. God said that if Israel walked in sin that the land would vomit them out just as it had the inhabitants before them[22].

Under the Law, there were still things that no representative sacrifice could provide a means of forgiveness for. If someone murdered a person, then the ground was contaminated by the blood that was shed, and the only way that contamination could be removed was by the death of the guilty person[23]. Yet for all other things the only possibility of removing the contamination of sin other than the death of the sinner was through faith in the blood of the Redeemer. The only place that the blood could affect its cleansing for sin was at the altar of God. It was there at the altar that God would meet with man and deal with his sin. God, who was enthroned above the cherubim, would look down upon the blood that was placed upon the altar and see that the righteous judgment of death had been paid for the sins that were committed.

---

22 Lev 18:25, 28; 20:22; Ezek 36:17

23 Num 35:31, 33; Ex 21:14, 23; Deut 19:12

Physical Life

"Only be sure that you do not eat the blood: for the blood is the life; and you can not eat the life with the flesh."

-Deuteronomy 12:23

We learn that the life of the flesh is in the blood and that God gave the blood as the means to make reconciliation for the sins of man[24]. The blood's role is so significant and symbolic of a person's life that God described Abel's death in terms of his blood crying out[25]. It is with this in mind that we later learn that the blood represents both the life and the death of the animal that would be used to atone for a person's sins. The sin of a person was transferred to the representative offering, and then the animal was put to death. The blood of that animal was then used to make atonement for the sins of the person who offered it. This was ultimately made

[24] Lev 17:11; Gen 9:4
[25] Gen 4:10

perfectly clear when Christ Jesus bore our sins in His own body[26]. Our sins were transferred to Him, and His blood brought the life of God to us[27].

Blood is the life of the body. It has been recognized as the embodiment of life from antiquity. There are physiological and biochemical properties of the blood that speak of this life. The blood carries the breath of life to every living part of our bodies as it binds the needed oxygen to its hemoglobin and distributes it to every cell. The liquid fibrous substance we call blood is in essence the substance of our life. The properties of the blood extend beyond what even modern medicine can comprehend. Yet there are certain physiological, biochemical, and immunological things about blood that we can say with a relatively high degree of certainty. It is a complex matrix of red cells, white cells, and platelets. Through a mixture of complex proteins, every cell in our bodies are fed, nurtured, and protected. The blood carries the important properties of life that protect us from every foreign and infectious agent, providing us with a defense against the diseases that would otherwise kill us. The blood is not only protective, but also healing and purifying, as it supplies an even more complex matrix of B-cells, T-cells, and their products to heal and cleanse the cells of our bodies. Thus through the blood, we have been given the

---

[26] 1 Pet 2:24; Heb 9:28
[27] Jn 6:53-54

means by which the essentials of life are supplied to us as well as the means to remove every impurity and contaminant that would jeopardize our life.

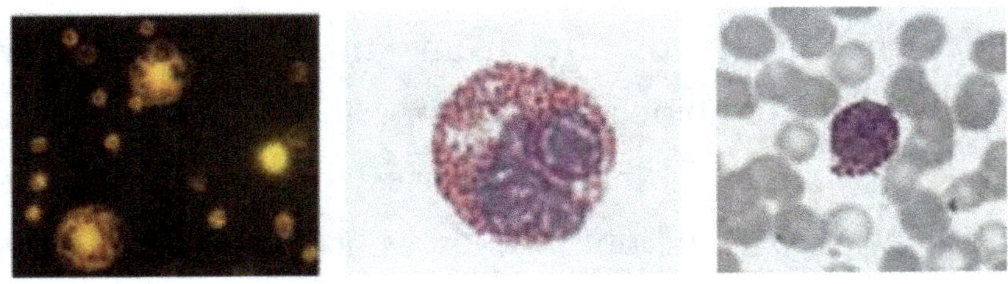

T-cells, eosinophils, and basophils are a few of the hundreds of healing and purifying properties in the blood

Spiritual Life

"And this is the witness that God has given us: eternal life – and this life is in His Son. He who has the Son has life, and he who does not have the Son of God does not have life."

-1 John 5:11-12

The equivalence of blood and life is underscored in ancient languages. Hebrew, Ugaritic, and Akkadian poetry grouped blood and life as lexical pairs[28]. Yet, the Bible takes the value of blood and extends it beyond natural life and makes it essential for spiritual life as well. Because the blood is the life of the flesh, it was the substance that would be used to intercede for man's spiritually dead and sinful state. The blood is referred to as the soul ('nephesh'), but only from the perspective that the soul represents the whole of an individual's life and being[29]. When the Bible speaks of the soul, it is usually referring to

---

28 Jacob Milgrom, Nov 1991
29 Gen 9:4; Lev 17:11; Deut 12:23

one's life as an individual. The blood of Jesus was in this respect His life, and His life was offered up for our redemption so that His life could be imparted to everyone who would believe[30].

It is only through the blood of Jesus that the life of God can be given to all men who are spiritually dead[31]. Only through the blood of Jesus can the stain of sin be cleansed, the soul be purified from its horrible disease, and the life of God restored[32]. The Almighty God cannot interact with sinful men – therefore, a remedy for their sins was necessary. As long as sin and death are present, God will not have a relationship with mankind[33]. God's judgment was that sin must be paid for by the death of the sinner[34]. Since it was impossible for man to pay for his sin and live, God in His love paid for our sins with His own life. The disease of sin can only be cured by the life of Christ Jesus imparted into us. God made it possible for us to die through the death of Jesus and then live again through the power of His resurrection[35]. Through the act of red-emption, the life of Jesus Christ poured out into everyone who will receive His life given blood.

---

[30] Jn 6:51-58
[31] Rom 5:12, 19; 7:14, 17, 20, 24; Eph 2:1-3, 18; Col. 2:13
[32] Mt 26:28; Jn 6:53; 1 Jn 1:7, 9; Ac 20:28; Rom 5:9; Eph 1:7; Col 1:1; Rev 1:5
[33] Gen 3:24; Ex 19:12; Lev 22:9; Num 4:15, 20, 18:22; Ex 30:30; Heb 9:7
[34] Gen 2:17; Ezek 18:4, 20, 24; Rom 5:12; 6:16, 24; Jam 1:15
[35] Gal 2:20; Rom 6:6; Col 3:3; 2 Cor 5:14-15; Heb 4:12

Until the fullness of time would bring to pass the incarnation of God and the sacrificial body and blood of the Savior, certain animals were offered as a testimony of Him. There were many who understood that these animal offerings represented the Redeemer who would give His life that all might live through Him[36]. Through faith in the coming Redeemer, those like Noah and Abraham were allowed to worship God with the blood of a sacrificial lamb. Then God took it one step further by allowing Moses to enter into the realms of glory to show him more about the Redeemer and the Holy Place where God dwells. In this revelation, God showed Moses the Holy of Holies in Heaven and how His people, though not permitted to come in, could interact with Him. He revealed to Moses how He Himself would come and remove the sin and death that ruled over the life of all mankind. Through faith in the blood of the covenant, a place would be consecrated for God to dwell in the midst of His people Israel until the fulness of time when the Redeemer would come and ransom and purify men from their sins.

---

[36] Gal 4:4; Heb 10:5; Gen 22:4; Job 19:25; Jn 8:56

Cutting of the Covenant

"I cut a covenant with my eyes; how then shall I gaze at a maid."

-Job 31:1

Before proceeding any further on the offerings of blood, we must establish the meaning of a covenant. It's important to draw the distinction between a singular act of establishing a covenant and the ongoing and continual acts of the sacrificial offerings. There was a unique phrase that was used to describe the slaying of an animal to establish a covenant. Different from all of the other offerings that were used for worshipping God, the "cutting of the covenant" was only done once to establish an agreement – and more, a blood-oath – between two parties. There was certainly a unique blood-oath when God cut the covenant with Abram.

The phrase that describes cutting a covenant is first used between God and Abram, בַּיּ֣וֹם הַה֗וּא כָּרַ֧ת יְהוָ֛ה אֶת־ אַבְרָ֖ם בְּרִ֣ית ("On this day, Yehovah cut a covenant with

Abram").[37] The "cutting of the covenant" demanded a unique animal sacrifice. God said to Abram, "Take for Me a heifer of three years old, and a she-goat of three years old, and a ram of three years old, and a turtledove, and a young pigeon."[38] The uniqueness of this covenant was that the blood of the sacrifices represents God's own life instead of Abram's life. Furthermore, God bound Himself to the covenant oath while not requiring Abram to do so. Abram made the sacrifice on behalf of God and divided the sacrifices so that God Himself could pass through the midst of the sacrifices. These sacrifices represented God's own life and He consecrated Himself to fulfill the blood-oath.[39] God swore an oath that day to give Abram a seed. The seed would be realized in Isaac but even greater the Redeemer Christ Jesus, who would purchase us with His own blood, would come forth of His own loins.[40] God used a representative offering for His own blood to cut the covenant that one day He would come and offer His own blood for man's salvation.

The next time that the Bible describes God cutting a covenant with man is at Mount Sinai. This time, Moses was instructed to offer oxen for Burnt Offerings and Peace Offerings unto the Lord.[41] Moses then took the blood and

---

37 (Gen 15:18)
38 (Gen 15:9)
39 (Neh 9:8)
40 (Gen 15:4-5; Gal 3:16)
41 (Ex 24:5)

sprinkled half of it upon the altar built for the Lord and the other half on the people.[42] When Moses sprinkled the blood on the people, it was a covenant that was cut for the people. They were now pledging an oath that they would keep all the words spoken to them by God.[43] Whereas God has spoken of what He would do when He cut the covenant with Abram now He places the requirement on His people regarding what they are required to do.

In the cutting of the covenant of the Law God bound the people with an obligation to perform their part of the agreement. "Thus the ratification ceremony was, in effect, the pledging of their lives as a guarantee of obedience to the divine will" (Mendenhall and Herion 1992). God would do for Israel what had never been done for a people or a nation, if Israel would only obey the terms of the covenant. God's part in the covenant was further emphasized when the Lord appeared to Moses, He promised to כֹּרֵת בְּרִית "koret berit" (cut a covenant) before all of the people of Israel and to do wonderful things that had never been done in the Earth.[44]

God had first cut (made) a covenant with Abram, but now it was with all of Israel. There were agreements and conditions set forth within the Sinai Covenant where not only was God vowing to be the God of Israel, but the people were also vowing to obey God as their God and

---

42 (Ex 24:6)
43 (Ex 24:3, 8; 34:27; Heb 9:19-20; 1 Ki 8:21; Jer 34:13)
44 (Ex 34:10)

King. The relationship that God had with Israel changed once the covenant was put into place. This change in relationship was witnessed by the difference between the way God treated Israel on the way to Sinai and the way He treated them after they left Sinai. When they murmured and complained about food and water on the way to Sinai, they were not held responsible for their actions. However, when they left Sinai, having been bound to the covenant, their murmuring and complaining was an act of rebellion against the One they had vowed to follow and obey. As a result, their wrong-doing was met with correction and judgment. Their obligations to the covenant were further emphasized in the blessings if they obeyed and the curses if they disobeyed.[45]

The cutting of a covenant does not necessarily include a blood sacrifice. "Běrît (covenent), came to be used to refer to many different types of oath-bound promises and relationships" (Mendenhall and Herion, 1992). Also, the cutting of a covenant can exist between individual men as well as between nations. There is even an example where a person cut a covenant with themself. Job said that he "cut a covenant" with his eyes not to behold a maid.[46] There were also several times that a covenant was cut as an act of a loyalty-oath, but there was no mention of a blood sacrifice.[47] Joshua brought all of Israel to reaffirm their

---

45 (Deut 28)
46 (Job 31:1)
47 (1 Sam 23:18; 2 Sam 3:12; 5:3; 1 Ki 5:12; Ezra 10:3; Neh 9:38 etc.)

commitment to God at Shechem,[48] and Jehoiada gathered the people to reaffirm their pledge to God – both cases were referred to as "cutting a covenant."[49] The greatest example of cutting a covenant as a loyalty pledge was observed with Josiah and the people of Israel.[50] Jeremiah described the covenant that was made by King Zedekiah and the leaders of Israel as "cutting a covenant." They cut a covenant to release the slaves, and thereby obey God's commandments.[51] They released them, but once the peril passed they then enslaved them again.[52] Although there was no mention of a blood-ritual – just an oath – Jeremiah made it equivalent to actually passing through the divided pieces of a blood sacrifice even as God did when He cut the covenant for Abram. God handing them over to destruction for cutting a covenant and not keeping it.[53]

One of the great examples of the responsibilities of cutting a covenant was witnessed at Gilgal. The Gibeonites deceived Joshua by disguising themselves as being from a far country. They desired to cut a covenant with the Israelites to avoid being attacked. Joshua cut the covenant and promised not to harm them, and later discovered that the Gibeonites were actually their neighbors.[54] After

---

[48] (Josh 24:25)
[49]
[50] (2 Ki 23:3)
[51] (Jer 34:8-9)
[52] (Jer 34:16)
[53] (Jer 34:17-20)
[54] (Josh 9:16)

cutting the covenant – which, by the way, was not described as having a blood-sacrifice involved – they were not able to annul it on any basis. Later, when the Gibeonites had been violated under the kingship of Saul, God held Israel responsible.

> *"Then there was a famine in the days of David three years, year after year, and David inquired of the LORD. And the LORD answered, "It is for Saul, and for his bloody house, because he slew the Gibeonites."*
>
> -2 Samuel 21:1

Because Israel, under Joshua, had "sworn" to them by a covenant, a "reconciliation" had to be made.[55] The reconciliation that was made could be considered a blood-sacrifice, because the Gibeonites hanged seven of Saul's sons as an atonement for the violation.[56]

Finally, there was a unique covenant of blood that God required all the males of Israel participate in: the covenant of circumcision.[57] This is the one covenant that God was very specific about being a covenant "between Me and you."[58] The strictness that God had for this covenant being observed was expressed when the son of Moses, Gershom, was singled out.

---

[55] (2 Sam 21:2,3)
[56] (2 Sam 21:9)
[57] (Gen 17:10)
[58] (Gen 17:10)

> *"And it came to pass by the way in the inn, that the LORD met him and sought to kill him. Then Zipporah took a sharp stone, and cut off the foreskin of her son, and cast it at his feet, and said, 'Surely a bloody husband you are to me.' So He let him go. Then she said, 'A bloody husband you are to me, because of the circumcision.'"*
>
> -Exodus 4:24–26

Circumcision remained a central feature of covenant relationship and consecration to the Lord from Abram to the end of the Covenant of the Law.[59]

---

[59] (Josh 5:7-8; Jn 7:22-23; Php 3:5)

The Judgment Against Sin

"[A]dultery, sexual immorality, uncleanness, lasciviousness, idolatry, magic, enmity, strife, jealousies, rage, rivalry, dissension, heresies, envy, intoxication, reveling, and things like this – as I have forewarned you, as also I told you before, that they who practice such things will not inherit the Kingdom of God."

-Gal 5:19-21

God is the Author of life. He has nothing whatsoever to do with death or sin. God is holy and separate from all evil. God is pure and holy – there is no sin or unrighteousness in Him. Any theology that has God as the Creator of sin is opposed to the revelation that God has given of Himself in Scripture. God has placed a judgment on all sin and iniquity: death.[60] Sin has its origin in the free will of the angels who God created. Lucifer rebelled against God, and God placed him and all of the

[60] (Gen 2:17; Rom 5:12; 6:23)

angels who followed him in a realm of darkness to await their final judgment. God also gave Adam a choice and made it very clear that disobedience would result in death. Adam chose to disobey and the result was spiritual death.

Spiritual death is a realm that is ruled by the first one who disobeyed and rebelled against God: Lucifer, also called Satan and the Devil. When Adam disobeyed and rebelled against God's Word, he came under the dominion of sin and death. Sin and the realm of darkness are entirely separated from God, and thus man became separated from God in his spiritual death. God in His mercy provided a Redeemer who would pay the penalty for sin and ransom man from the power and realm of darkness. God's testimony of the coming Redeemer was established in the offering of an innocent animal sacrifice that would represent the life of God, Christ Jesus. The sacrifice was all revealing how exceedingly sin was and the need for redemption. Every sacrifice pointed to the One who would come and return the life of God that was lost by sin. God would come and shed His own blood to purchase man's salvation. He would incur the full judgment of mankind's sin by bearing it all in His own body. With His own blood He would cleanse man from their sins and restore the life of God to all who were willing to believe.

In the realm of sin and death there was no way to interact with God other than to express faith in the coming Redeemer by offering a sacrifice for sins. It was a sacrifice that represented the life of the person who offered it. By the offering of the sacrifice, men would recognize that they were sinners and that their sins could only be dealt with by their death. Through the mediation of the sacrifice God made it possible for the worshipper to interact with Himself. This interaction was first demonstrated through Adam's son, Abel. However always at the heart of every sacrifice God pointed to the One who would bear the sins of many,

> *"But he was wounded for our transgressions, He was bruised for our iniquities: The chastisement of our peace was upon him; And with his stripes we are healed. All we like sheep have gone astray; We have turned every one to his own way; And the LORD hath laid on him the iniquity of us all."*
>
> -Isaiah 53:5–6

The blood of the sacrificial offerings could not take away sin from the heart of men, but it could offer a means of reconciliation. Just as a covenant could not be ratified without the death of the sacrificial offering, neither could the sin be temporarily dealt with unless a sacrifice was offered.[61] Without the shedding of blood, there could be no forgiveness for sin.[62] God established the means by which a whole nation could fellowship with Him through

---

61 (Heb 9:17)
62 (Heb 9:22)

the covenant of Sinai. Paul described the covenant of Sinai as bondage, because it could never deliver men from their sins.[63] It could never change their hearts or impart the life of God.[64] Much like the birth of Ishmael, it was still a substitute for the promise of the coming Seed.[65] It was weak because it depended upon men, who were bound by a nature of sin.[66] It would not be until the promised Seed would come that sin could truly be removed and the life of God imparted.[67]

Sin is one of the most common subjects of the Bible in both the Old and New Covenants. Everywhere sin is found, the judgment of God against it is declared. The word for "sin" and its synonyms like "iniquity," "wickedness," and "transgression" are found in more than 1,700 passages of Scripture. All disobedience to the ways of God is sin. The opposite of sin is righteousness, even as the opposite of wrong is right. The evidence of sin and its consequences is not elusive. The definition and description of sin could not be more detailed and leaves no room for interpretation. Sin began with Adam and has been evident in every human being until this day. All have sinned and all live under the reign of the spirit of disobedience if they have not been washed in the blood

---

63 (Gal 3:10; Rom 7:7-23; 8:3)
64 (Gal 3:21)
65 (Gal 4:24)
66 (Rom 8:3; Heb 7:18; Rom 7:7-25)
67 (Gen 3:20; Gal 3:19, 21; Tt 3:5)

and born again.[68] Sin, which is disobedience against the ways of God, results in separation from God. Only God can provide a means of forgiving men of their sins and the means of delivering them from the judgment of death. The only means by which sin can be atoned for and ultimately cleansed is by faith in the blood of the Redeemer.

---

68 (Eph 2:2; Rom 3:23)

The Altar
The Meeting Place

"This shall be a continual burnt offering throughout your generations at the door of the tabernacle of the congregation before the LORD: where I will meet you, to speak there unto you"

-Exodus 29:42

The Altars of Man

Altars were built as a place to meet with God. The Hebrew word for "altar," מִזְבֵּחַ ('mizbeach') is derived from the Hebrew verbal root זבח ('zavach'), which means "to slaughter" and thus denotes that altars were made to pour out the blood of the sacrifice so that the just payment for sin could be acknowledged and so that men could thereby worship God. Altars could be built of stone or of earth to offer the burnt offerings and peace offerings.[69] The first altar that was built seems to have been built by

69 (Ex 20:24-26; Deut 27:5-7; Jdg 13:15-20; 1 Sam 6:14-15)

Abel the son of Adam, but no mention of the construction of an altar was given. Noah was the first person that the Bible definitely describes as having built an altar.[70] The specific purpose was to worship God by offering those offerings just as Abel did which represented the blood of the Lamb. These offerings would ascend into Heaven and afford man the privilege of interacting with God. God responded to Abel's offering and referred to him both as a prophet and one who was righteous.[71] God responded to the offering of Noah and made a covenant with Him.[72] The only indication that we have concerning how man received the revelation of offering these animals to the Lord is found in Genesis 3.[73] Adam and Eve watched as God made provision to clothe their shame and nakedness by making garments of animal hides.[74] Obviously, in order for God to have made Adam and Eve coats of skins, He would have had to kill an animal. It stands therefore to reason that God would have demonstrated through this act the testimony of the Savior who was slain from the "overthrow"/"foundation" (καταβολή, 'katabole'), of mankind.[75]

Abraham built several altars to God. Abraham did not call on the name of God unless it was at the altar- the

---

[70] (Gen 8:20)
[71] (Mt 35:35; Lk 11:50-51; Heb 11:4)
[72] (Gen 8:20-9:17; Heb 9:16)
[73] (Heb 11:4-17)
[74] (Gen 3:15, 21)
[75] (Lk 11-50-51; Rev 13:8)

place of communion.[76] We are able to gain insight to the intercession that was made at the altar of burnt offerings when we look at Abraham's offering of Isaac.[77] It was at this time that we observed a step by step act of worship from the preparation of the offering to the building of the altar. The offering that God had chosen was identified and consecrated to the Lord. At the moment of consecration the offering no longer belonged to man but was transferred from the human realm to the divine. The next step was for Abraham to build the altar of stone to transfer the offering from the material realm to the spiritual. The wood was laid upon the altar, the sacrifice was then tied, and the body was placed on top of the wood. Before the fire was lit Abraham prepared to kill the sacrifice with a

[76] (Gen 12:8; 13:4; 22:9)
[77] (Gen 22:9)

knife so that the blood would flow out upon the altar. After the blood of the sacrifice poured out upon the altar the fire was lit and the offering would be burned in the fire so that it could ascend into Heaven as the intercession to worship God. Although Abraham had prophesied that the LORD would provide the sacrifice it was at this time that one of the greatest revelations of God's coming Redeemer was revealed.[78]

> *"And Abraham said, 'My son, God will provide Himself a Lamb for a burnt offering.'"*
>
> -Genesis 22:8

God reached out in His grace and revealed the sacrificial Lamb that He would provide not only to bless Abraham but all of the nations of the Earth. If this was not the greatest revelation to Abraham of the Redeemer who would become his sacrifice for sin it certainly was one of the foremost. Jesus said, "Your father Abraham rejoiced to see My day, and he saw it and was glad."[79]

Isaac also built an altar to the Lord after the Lord had appeared to him in Beersheba.[80] Jacob set up a pillar after the Lord appeared to him in Bethel and thereby dedicated a house to God.[81] Afterward, he would return to this same

---

[78] (Gen 22:8, 17; Gal 3:16)
[79] (Jn 8:56)
[80] (Gen 26:25)
[81] (Gen 28:18-22)

place and build an altar by the direction of the LORD.[82] Later, Moses would build an altar in Rephidim and at Horeb; Balaam in Moab; Joshua on Mount Ebal; the Reubenites, Gadites, and Manassehites at Trans-jordan; Gideon at Ophra; David's family in Bethlehem; David at the threshing floor of Araunah; Elijah at Mt. Carmel; and Zerubbabel in Jerusalem.[83] All of these altars were for the blood of the whole burnt offerings to atone for sin and means to interact with, worship and honor God.

---

[82] (Gen 35:1, 7)

[83] (Ex 17:15, 24:2; Num 23:1, 14, 29; Josh 8:30-31; Deut 27:4-7; Josh 22:10-16; 1 Sam 20:6, 29; 2 Sam 24:25; 1 Ki 18:30; Ezra 3:2)

The Brazen Altar

"And Solomon went up from there to the brazen altar before the LORD, which was at the tabernacle of the congregation, and offered a thousand burnt offerings upon it."

-2 Chronicles 1:6

Once the covenant at Sinai was established, God had Moses build a new kind of altar for whole-burnt offerings. There would also be a unique emphasis placed on how the blood would be manipulated upon it or its foundation. It was at this time that God would not just meet with a single person but with a whole nation. It would be upon the Brazen Altar that the continual burnt offering would be offered. The whole burnt offering would be offered every evening and morning.[84] Once again, it is here that we gain insight to the oldest offering mentioned in the Bible: the whole-burnt offering.

---

84 (Ex 29:38-43)

It was upon this altar that the fire came down out of Heaven and consumed the offering. The fire that came from Heaven was to never go out.[85]

> *"And there came a fire out from before the LORD, and consumed upon the altar the burnt offering and the fat, which when all the people saw, they shouted and fell on their faces."*
>
> -Leviticus 9:24

[85] (Lev 6:5; 12-13; 9:24)

> "The fire shall always be burning upon the altar; it shall never go out."
>
> -Leviticus 6:13

> "Here the word 'tāmîd' stresses the importance of maintaining the fire even if the sacrifices are totally consumed." "...and it is this fire which is not allowed to die out so that all subsequent sacrifices might claim divine acceptance" (Jacob Milgrom, 2008).

> "The law says, "A fire shall be kept burning on the altar which shall never be extinguished, but shall be kept burning for ever" (Charles Duke Yonge 1995).

It was from this perpetual fire that the incense was lit on fire and the lights of the menorah burned. There was no other source of fire allowed to burn in ministering to God except the fire that came down from Heaven. If any other fire was brought into the Tabernacle of the LORD, it was considered "strange fire." It was for this reason that Aaron's sons, Nadab and Abihu, were slain by the fire of God.

The opportunity to meet with God was expanded to anyone - no matter who they were - in the nation of Israel. God invited all of Israel to come and meet with Him at the door of the Tabernacle.[86] The brazen altar stood first at the door of the "Tent of Meeting"

---

[86] (Lev 1: 2)

(Tabernacle) in the wilderness and then was later positioned in the courtyard just outside of the Temple.[87] Every offering would be killed before the brazen altar. The blood of these offerings would be carried inside of the Tabernacle on Yom Kippur to remove the sin that contaminated the altars of God. It would be through the application of the blood upon the altar that the past sins of Israel would be removed so that God could continue to dwell in the midst of Israel. This is yet another witness to the need for blood to remove the contamination of sin any time the act is committed.[88]

On the day of Pentecost, God sent the divine fire of the Holy Spirit that rested upon the heads of everyone gathered in the upper room.[89] The blood had been received and applied to their lives on the night of the Passover meal when Jesus said, this is my blood of the new covenant, which is shed for many for the remission of sins.[90] Now when Pentecost came the divine fire of the Holy Spirit came upon the offerings that were holy and acceptable to God. When the fire of the Holy Spirit came the Holy Spirit filled them and became ruler of their lives. At that moment the Holy Spirit empowered the disciples with the power to be witnesses of the resurrection life of Jesus Christ. The fire empowered them to be those who

---

87 (Ex 27:1-8; 38:1-7; 2 Chron 4:1)
88 (Ex 29:36; 30:10; Lev 4:1-5, 13-15; 16:19; 1 Jn 1:9)
89 (Ac 2:4)
90 (Mt 26:28)

worshiped in Spirit and truth. The fire that fell upon them produced within them the life and outworking of God that could only be likened to rivers- for the greatness and magnitude of it. Every dimension of what is pleasing to God came by the fire of the Holy Spirit. This fire of the Holy Spirit is for service, for worship, for prayer, for every dimension of the light of the Gospel to shine from our lives. Any other fire that is not the working of the Holy Spirit is "strange fire."

The Altars of the Sanctuary

"Who serve as a model and shadow of the heavenlies, according as Moses was divinely instructed when he was about to complete the tabernacle, 'for see,' says He, 'that you make all things according to the pattern that was shown you in the mountain.'"

-Hebrews 8:5

The sanctuary that Moses built was a copy and shadow of the heavenly one.[91] Therefore, everything that was inside of the sanctuary represented what God was doing in Heaven and revealed how mankind would be allowed to come into the heavenly realm. There would be no sacrifices offered inside of the sanctuary. The only thing that would be brought into the sanctuary pertaining to the sacrifices was the blood of the sin offerings.

There are divisions of sacredness taught to us in the design of the tabernacle. The innermost room where the Ark of the Testimony was placed would be where God

---

91 (Heb 8:5; Ex 25:40; Rev 11:19)

would visit the people of Israel. It was the holiest place of all consecrated only to the Lord – a place that only the high priest could come into once a year. However, the high priest could not enter without the prescribed blood that represented the blood of Christ Jesus.[92] He could not come in unless every part of his being represented "holiness unto the LORD." From the crown upon his head all the way down to the innermost garments upon his body. In this absolute identity of holiness the high priest would enter into the innermost forbidden chamber and remove the sins of the people that had contaminated God's dwelling place.[93]

The holy place which was the chamber just before the veil of the Holy of Holies, but still within the sanctuary, was where the priests were allowed to do the service of God's house. It was a place where the priest had to be endowed with a special anointing of holiness and consecration in order to be permitted to do this service. Knowing that the sanctuary was a sketch of the heavenly sanctuary we can grasp the idea that this was actually a heavenly ministry that they were engaged in as they took care of the table of bread, the menorah and the golden altar of incense.[94] To walk around in the sanctuary of God, they had to be holy unto the LORD, which God made

---

92 (Heb 9:6-12; 10:1, 11-13)
93 (Lev 16:8, 15-16; Ex 25:22; 29:42-43)
94 (Ex 25:40; Ac 7:44; Heb 8:5)

possible through the blood that was upon them.[95] They had been consecrated which is to say they had already been transferred from the realm of men to the realm of God. Now, belonging wholly to God they were able to minister in the sanctuary of God. Still even though they were given this special holiness, they were still unable to come in behind the veil, which was the most holy place of all. It was there that God would be enthroned upon His mercy seat. It was here that God would dwell in the midst of His people. Although He would dwell among His people He had to remain separated from them which the veil signified. All the blood that was offered as a provision for sin could not remove the sin that contaminated their soul. Although provision was made to forgive the sin a separation still existed between God and man. This separation would remain until the Redeemer came and removed the sin and thereby removed the veil of separation![96]

God had made a way to come and dwell in the midst of His people that were spiritually dead in their trespasses and sins. However, it was imperative that they realize that they were unable to truly fellowship with Him because of the nature and power of sin that still had dominion over them. They were allowed to come only so close and then they would see the images that would remind them of the

---

95 (Ex 29:20-21; Lev 8:23-24, 30)

96 (Num 7:89; 17:8; Ex 25:21-22; Heb 9:4)

words, "draw not nigh!"[97] The veil was embroidered with figures of cherubim, a reminder that sinful man was not allowed back into the presence of God.[98] The fellowship that man had of walking with God in the paradise of His glory was lost. However, through a strict mediation by the priest in accordance with the Law, God would dwell with them. It would not be possible to speak more to the evil and destructive consequence of sin than to observe the rivers of blood that flowed to mediate for man's sin until the time of the Redeemer.

When Jesus – whose very life represented that veil – died as the sin offering at Calvary, the veil was torn from top to bottom, providing all of mankind who would believe with the holiness and purity required to live in the place where God dwells.[99] The Holies of Holies was not done away with when Jesus gave us His life by pouring out His blood through death – rather, the power of death and sin that barred man's entrance was destroyed. There are no longer cherubim guarding the way to prohibit our entering into this wonderful and sacred realm. There is no longer the voice of our heavenly Father saying, "draw not nigh." Now we may come with all boldness into the Holy of Holies, having been washed with the blood of the Lamb.[100] The veil that we walk through now is the body of

---

[97] (Ex 3:5; 19:12)
[98] (Gen 3:24; Ex 26:1, 31)
[99] (Mt 27:5; Heb 9:8)
[100] (Heb 10:19)

our Lord Jesus Christ, the Savior of the world! The first tabernacle has been removed, (the holy place), the Holy Spirit now signifying that the way into the Holiest place of all is open to us.[101] Now through the blood of Jesus Christ, we come directly into the Holy of Holies where Father dwells, and we come with all boldness by the blood of Jesus.[102]

---

[101] (Heb 9:2-8)
[102] (Heb 10:19-22)

The Golden Altar of Incense

"And another angel came and stood at the altar, having a golden censer, and a lot of incense was given to him so that he might offer the prayers of all the saints upon the golden altar which was before the throne. And the smoke of the incense went up with the prayers of the saints out of the hand of the angel before God."

-Revelation 8:3-4

The golden altar of incense was directly in front of the second sanctuary, the Holy of Holies, and flanked by the menorah and the table of bread.[103] Just like the whole burnt offering that was offered every evening and morning even so the incense was to be offered every evening and morning.[104] The incense was also an essential part of going into the second tabernacle, before the Ark of the Covenant during the purification on Yom Kippur. If

---

103 (Ex 30:1-10; 37:25-28; 40:5; 1 Ki 7:20-21, 48)
104 (Ex 30:7-8)

the cloud of incense was not present when the blood was applied to the mercy seat, then the high priest would die.[105] The incense represented both the intercession of God's priest and the intercession that would ultimately be made by Christ Jesus and the Holy Spirit.

The first death that took place over the mishandling of the sacred things of God took place around the offering of incense. Their mishandling of the incense was called the offering of "strange fire." "Nadab and Abihu, the sons of Aaron, took either of them his censer, and put fire therein, and put incense thereon, and offered strange fire before

105 (Lev 16:13)

the LORD, which he commanded them not".[106] Coals from off of the altar were placed in the censors and then the incense that God had formulated were placed upon the coals. The incense was offered up by holy fire, a fire that came from God and was touched by the blood of the sacrifices. The coals that burnt upon the altar were holy and even had the power to impart holiness. The seraphim were commanded by God to take coals from off the altar so that the sins and iniquities of the profit Isaiah could be purged.[107] Instead of the holy fire they offered strange fire which would have been a fire from another source than that which belonged to God. Although there have been many speculations about this particular act, the one fact that we are confronted with was their disobedience. They failed to follow the specific instruction given to them by God. Through their deviation from the instructions of God, they violated the holiness that was provided to them by the grace of God and were struck down by the fire of God. The only fire that was allowed in the ministry of the temple and ministry to God was the fire that God provided when He set the sacrifice on fire.

The only people that were allowed into the holy place where the golden altar of incense was were the priests sanctified to minister there. Unlike the Holy of Holies, there were daily activities in this area of the first sanctuary.

---

[106] (Le 10:1; Ex 30:9)
[107] (Isa 6:7)

The altar of incense was tended to twice daily by the priest so that there would be a continual offering going up before the LORD.[108] There were to be no burnt offerings, bread offerings, or drink offerings offered upon this altar.[109] This altar was all about a different kind of offering – one that represented a continual intercession and fellowship with the LORD. The altar of incense was seen in Heaven in the book of Revelation as the place where the prayers of the saints are continually offered up before the LORD.[110]

108 (Ex 30:7-8)
109 (Ex 30:9)
110 (Rev 8:3-5)

The Ark of the Covenant

"And make one cherub on the one end, and the other cherub on the other end: even of the mercy seat shall you make the cherubim on the two ends. And the cherubim shall stretch forth their wings on high, covering the mercy seat with their wings, and their faces shall look one to another; toward the mercy seat shall the faces of the cherubim be. And you shall put the Mercy Seat above upon the Ark; and in the Ark you shall put the testimony that I shall give you. And there I will meet with you, and I will commune with you from above the Mercy Seat, from between the two cherubim which are upon the ark of the testimony, of all things which I will give you in commandment unto the children of Israel."

-Exodus 25:19–22

The most important altar of all was the altar that represented the throne of God. The Ark of the Covenant was kept in the Holies of Holies where the LORD's presence dwelt. Only *one* person, the high priest, was allowed in this most holy place, and that was *once* a year. The high priest came in before the presence of the LORD for the sole purpose of decontaminating the Ark from the sins of the people that had defiled it.[111] There is much that can be said about the symbolic nature of the Ark of the Covenant, but most specific to our discussion here is the lid of the Ark (the mercy seat). It is the lid of the Ark that we would consider as an altar, for it was here that the blood was applied.

Of all the altars and places of worship, this is the most holy of all, for it was here where God would come and manifest His glory. Only one person was allowed to enter into this area and draw near to this altar: the high priest.

---

[111] (Lev 16:16)

Unlike all other men, the high priest was given a special anointing of holiness so that he would be enabled to interact with God on behalf of all mankind. His status of holiness before God was absolutely essential and was highlighted by the crown that was given to him to wear that declared that he was, "Holiness Unto the LORD."[112]

The Mercy Seat (כַּפֹּרֶת, 'kapporet') was the most unique altar of the Old Testament. This particular word carries great meaning and insight with regards to the redemption that we have received by Christ Jesus. The mercy seat, which was made of pure gold, was the lid of the Ark of the Covenant.[113] It was here that God would appear in His glory cloud once a year during the time of purgation.[114] Yet at the same time, it was also the place where God's voice could be heard throughout the year, as He would make known His will to the high priest.[115] It was for this reason that the Holy of Holies was also called the דְּבִיר ('devir') and translated is as "oracle," the place where God's instructions were heard.[116]

It was the abiding presence of the Almighty God that made the Holy of Holies the special place that it was. Whenever God's presence was there the Holy of Holies was filled with His holiness and glory. Just as no one could

---

112 (Ex 39:30)
113 (Ex 26:34)
114 (Lev 16:2)
115 (Ex 25:22; 30:6; Num 7:89)
116 (1 Ki 6:16, 19-23; 7:49; 8:6-8; 2 Chron 5:7)

come near the mountain when God's presence had descended upon Mount Sinai, neither could anyone come into the Holy of Holies except one person: the high priest, who had been given a special anointing and holiness to stand before the "בְּחַי הָעוֹלָם" the Living One.[117]

The Mercy Seat was viewed as a replica of the throne of God.[118] It has been noted that in the enlarged version of the cherubim scene in the temple that Solomon built in 2 Chronicles 3:10-13, the wings formed a place for the invisible God to sit. The outspread wings of the cherubim form a throne for God, and the lid of the ark being a footstool for the throne. King David appears to refer to the lid itself as the floor of the throne room or the footstool of God.[119]

> "This cultic assemblage is closely associated with what Mettinger sees as the "original and complete title" ṣĕbāʾôt yōšēb hakkĕrūbîm, (The LORD of hosts who dwells between the cherubim) in which the central expression for the divine presence is the word yašab" (dwells) (Thomas W. Mann, 1984).

It was there, between the cherubim, where God would speak to the people of Israel.[120]

---

[117] (Lev 16:2; Ex 19:8, 21, 24; Heb 12:20; Dan 12:7)
[118] (2 Sam 6:2; 1 Chron 13:6; 1 Sam 4:4; Ps 99:11; Isa 37:16)
[119] (1 Chron 28:2; Ps 99:5; 132:7)
[120] (Ex 25:22; Num 7:89; 1 Sam 4:4; 2 Sam 6:2 etc)

> *"And when Moses had gone into the tabernacle of the congregation to speak with Him, then he heard the voice of One speaking to him from off the Mercy Seat that was upon the ark of testimony, from between the two cherubim, and He spoke to him."*
>
> -Numbers 7:89

Once again, this emphasizes why the Holy of Holies was also called the דְּבִיר ('devir,' ("oracle"), because it was the place where God's word was heard.[121]

When Ezekiel saw the throne of God descending upon the temple, he saw something that was very similar to the imagery on the Ark. In Ezekiel's encounter with the throne of God, God was over the heads of the cherubim as He sat enthroned upon them. He also saw in between the midst of the cherubim, where the blood was applied by the high priest, coals of fire.[122]

---

121 (1 Ki 6:5, 16-31)
122 (Ezek 10:1-4; 18-19; 11:22)

The Altars: where men met with God and sin was dealt with

The First Type of Altar- Whole Burn Offerings

The Ark of The Covenant **The Altar of Incense** **The Brazen Altar**

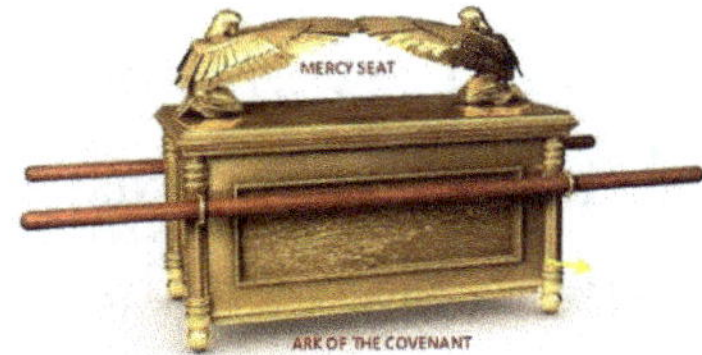

The Last and Final Altar- The Cross of Christ

Blood To Cleanse the Altars

"For the life of the flesh is in the blood: and I have given it to you upon the altar to make reconciliation for your souls; for it is the blood that makes reconciliation for the soul."

-Leviticus 17:11

Depending upon the type of sin and the person who sinned, the blood was manipulated in different ways. Some sin was so potent that it reached into the Holy Place inside God's tent. If the priest or the entire community of Israel sinned, then the blood had to be applied to both the Altar of Incense and the Brazen Altar.[123] If an individual, including a leader, sinned, then the blood was only applied to the Brazen Altar.[124] However, the most severe sins polluted even the Holy of Holies, and specifically the Ark of the Covenant. The sins of the people would contaminate the place where they met with God, and until

---

123 (Lev 4:2-21)
124 (Lev 4:22-35)

the sin was dealt with, the fellowship was hindered. The Holy of Holies exemplified this more than the other altars: the presence of the LORD would not come until the sin was removed. The only way that the sin could be removed from the altar was by the application of the blood.[125]

> "...the function of all of the blood manipulations becomes clear: to purge the sanctuary of its accumulated pollution" (Jacob Milgrom, 2008).

> "All year long, Israel's sins have been polluting the sanctuary. True, the pious have been bringing purification offerings, which prove effective because their impurity was caused inadvertently. However, what of the advertent, brazen sinner? Their sins have penetrated into the adytum, the inner sanctum, polluting the very seat of the Godhead, threatening the destruction of the community" (Jacob Milgrom, 2004).

We understand that the sins that were dealt with on a daily basis throughout the year were atoned for at the Brazen altar. The sin was stopped at the altar so that it could proceed no further - otherwise, it entered into the tabernacle. However, those sins that the people refused to repent of affected the very presence of God in their midst. Those continual and unrepented sins reached all the way

---

[125] (Lev 16:16, 33)

into the Holy of Holies and contaminated the dwelling place of God and could only be taken care of on Yom Kippur, the Day of Purgation! The application of the blood cleansed the Holy of Holies and God's presence would return to dwell in the midst of His people.

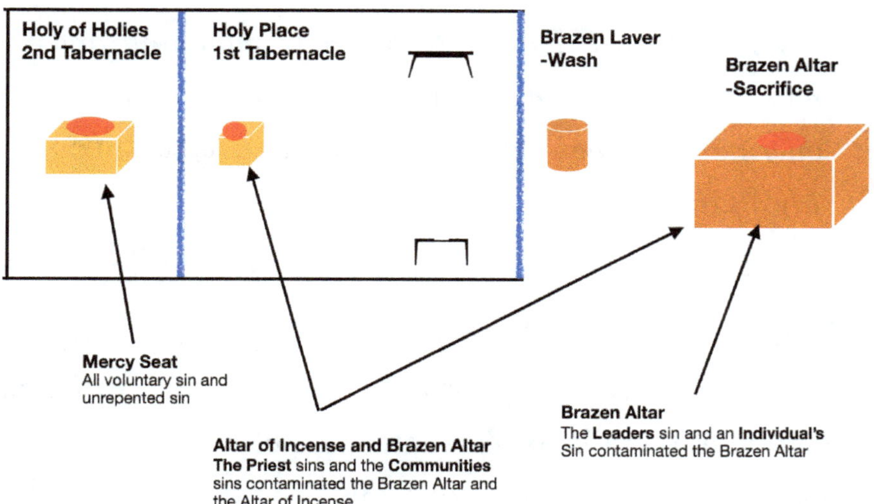

Sacrificial Offerings

"Even them will I bring to My holy mountain and make them joyful in My house of prayer. Their burnt offerings and their sacrifices shall be accepted upon My altar;"

-Isaiah 56:7.

There were primarily nine sacrificial offerings given to Israel to cleanse, purify, protect, sanctify, and worship. Each one of them involved some form of manipulation of blood (except for the meal offering). The treatment of the sacrifice was determined based upon how the blood was used. The ritual of the offerings usually followed a prescribed order: first the sin-offering, then the burnt-offering, and finally the peace-offering.[126] First, there must be an atonement for sin, then the consecration of oneself (the whole-Burnt Offering), and finally the Fellowship-Offerings, such as the Peace-Offering.[127]

---

126 (Num 6:16-17; Ex 29:10-18; Lev 8:1-29; 2 Chron 29:20-36)
127 (Deut 12:17-19)

Nine Sacrificial Offerings

Some of the sacrifices such as the Passover, Peace, Thanksgiving, Meal, and Freewill-Offerings were eaten as testimony to communion with God. The Burnt-Offering was more reflective of worship and adoration of God, but was also used to atone for sin. It was the oldest of the offerings and was also used to commemorate something that God had done. Finally, the Sin-Offering, Guilt (trespass) Offering, and the Yom Kippur offerings were used to remove the uncleanness caused by sin. Of all of these offerings, the most diverse offering was the sin offering, whose blood was manipulated differently based upon the type of sin and the status of the individual. Below is a brief summary of these offerings:

1- The Passover-Offering: The first time the Passover-Offering was offered, a male lamb without blemish was slain, its blood was applied to the door of the house (lintel and doorpost), and the sacrifice was eaten in communion with the Lord. All of the offering had to be eaten with nothing left for the next day. In preparation for the Passover, all leaven had to be removed from a person's dwelling. Afterward, it was offered once a year on the 14th of Nisan and eaten toward the evening.[128] It is this offering that was most closely associated with Christ Jesus as the Lamb of God who was slain on Passover.

2- Peace-Offering: The Peace-Offering, which would be understood as a Fellowship-Offering, could be a lamb or a goat, male or female, and without blemish. It had to be killed at the door of the tabernacle while the offerer laid his hand upon it. The blood was sprinkled around the brazen altar. The inward parts were burned upon the altar, and the flesh was eaten in communion with the Lord.[129] The Peace-Offering also included the Wave -Offering, which the Priest waved before the Lord, and he would eat it on behalf of the Lord.

3- Thanksgiving-Offering: The Thanksgiving-Offering was offered like the Peace Offering but with unleavened cakes and leavened bread. The flesh of the Peace Offering must be eaten the same day. Like the Passover offering, nothing can be left for the next day.[130]

4- Meal-Offering: The Meal-Offering was an offering of flour mixed with oil and frankincense, or unleavened cakes anointed with oil baked or fired in a pan. The oil, as symbolic of the Holy Spirit and the anointing, took the place of the blood.[131] The priest offered a handful upon the altar, or a portion of the cakes, and burned them upon

---

[128] (Ex 12:1-20)
[129] (Lev 3)
[130] (Lev 7:12-14)
[131] (1 Jn 5:8)

the altar. There is a strict prohibition not to offer any leaven or honey upon God's altar. These offerings must be offered with salt. The remainder belongs to the priest – it's a most holy offering. Any first-fruits offering has to include the Meal-Offering.[132]

5- Freewill-Offering: The Freewill Offering might also be called a voluntary Peace-Offering. There were some unique things about the Freewill-Offering. The Freewill-Offering could be made of the cattle or the sheep. What was unique about these offerings is that they could consist of animals that had blemishes. However if the animal had a blemish, it could not be offered upon the altar.[133]

6- Burnt-Offering: Although the Burnt-Offering is the oldest of all the types of offerings, its first introduction after the establishment of the Sinai Covenant is found in Leviticus 1, which includes the hand-leaning rite. The animals used for sacrifice were a bull calf and a male lamb or goat without blemish. The blood was sprinkled around the base of the brazen altar. It was cut into pieces, and the head and the fat were laid upon the wood, but the inward parts and the legs were washed with water, and then it was all burned upon the altar. The Burnt-Offering may also be of turtledoves or pigeons and also as a Meal-Offering. The Meal-Offerings were also included in the burnt offerings and were to be handled by the priest as described

---

132 (Lev 2)
133 (Lev 7:16; 22:18, 23)

previously. The remainder of the Meal-Offering was to be eaten by the priest with unleavened bread in a holy place in the court of the tabernacle, which is all testifying of communion with God. In addition to the Meal-Offerings were the Drink-Offerings that were poured out with the sacrifices. There are also the regulations concerning the morning and evening Burnt-Offerings, and the offerings that burn all night upon the altar. The ashes of these sacrifices were holy and had to be carried by the priest to a clean place outside the camp. The evening and the morning sacrifice were to be offered every day, and the fire upon the altar was never to go out. All of the offerings unto the Lord were "most holy" or "holy of holies" (קֹדֶשׁ הַקֳּדָשִׁים, 'qodesh haqodashem').[134]

7- The Sin Offering: The Sin-Offering is most holy before the Lord. It was to be offered any time a person sinned in any way against the Lord. There were different animals required depending on a person's rank and status in the community. Whatever the animal was – whether bull calf, lamb, or goat – the offerer had to lay his hand upon the animal, which implies a confession, and then the sacrifice was killed on the north side of the altar before the Lord. The blood was then sprinkled seven times before the Brazen Altar (Altar of Burnt-Offering). The blood was also put on the horns of the Altar of Incense inside the Tabernacle. The remainder of blood was poured out at the

[134] (Lev 1:1-17; 6:8-13; Ex 29:38-42; Num 15:1-10; 28:1-10)

bottom of the Brazen Altar. Similarly to the Peace-Offering, the fat, kidneys, and offal are burned upon the altar. The remainder was taken outside the camp to a clean place and burned.[135]

8- The Guilt Offering: The Guilt-Offering was also most holy – it was much like the sin offering and was used to deal with the unclean state of a person. There is a special emphasis placed on the confession of the sin with the Guilt-Offering. The offering could be a female lamb, a male or female goat, or two turtledoves, or two pigeons, or an offering of fine flour with no oil or frankincense. The offering of the birds was special in that one was used for sin and the other in place of the inward parts of the animal was used for a burnt offering. There was also an additional trespass offering if one sinned by ignorance, which required both a ram for sacrifice and restitution money. Additionally, if a person carried any guilt at all, they were to offer a ram without blemish.[136]

9- The Yom Kippur Offering: The Yom Kippur Offering consisted first of the offering for the priest and then secondly of the special offerings of two goats. This is the one time that the High Priest would enter into the innermost chamber of the Tabernacle where the Mercy Seat was on the Ark of the Covenant. The High Priest had to first offer a bull calf for a Sin-Offering and a ram for a

---

135 (Lev 1:17; 4:12; Ezek 43:18-27)
136 (Lev 1:17; 5:1-6:7)

Burnt-Offering, which would make atonement for himself and his house. He would do this only after washing his body and putting on holy garments. Every part of this ritual was Holy of Holies, and there could be nothing that might cause uncleanness. He would then present two goats before the LORD. He would cast lots to determine which goat would be for the LORD and which one would be for the congregation of Israel. The blood of the goat for the LORD would be taken into the Holy of Holies and applied to the mercy seat to purify God's dwelling place from the sins of the people. The High Priest would place both hands on the second goat to transfer the sins of the people to it, and the goat would be sent away to Azazel in the wilderness while all of Israel watched their sins carried away to return no more.

The Chambers and Altars of the Tabernacle

"Now these things, having therefore been prepared, the priests entered at all times into the first tabernacle to accomplish their service. But into the second, the High Priest entered alone once a year, not without blood, which he offered for himself and for the people's sins committed in ignorance. By this the Holy Spirit signified that the way into the Holies was not yet revealed so long as the first tabernacle remained standing."

-Hebrews 9:6-9

The tabernacle was divided into two chambers. They were divided by a veil, which in Hebrew is called a 'parokhet.' The 'parokhet' divided the "holy place" (הַקֹּדֶשׁ) from the "most holy place" (קֹדֶשׁ הַקֳּדָשִׁים: 'qodesh haqodashem).' When we speak of 'qodesh haqodashem,' we understand that there can be nothing more sacred and absolutely nothing more dangerous. The Ark of the Covenant is in this inner chamber on which the 'kapporet' ("mercy seat") is found.[137] The 'parokhet' ("the veil") was adorned with cherubim, reminding us of those stationed at the entrance to the garden of Eden to prevent man's return into that place of communion with God. On the other hand, the curtain that separated the holy place from the outside was made of the same multi-color fabric as the 'parokhet,' but was not woven with cherubim. The priest would pass through this curtain every day in their administration of the things of the holy place. As they ministered to God at the altar of incense, the table of bread, and the menorah.

Just outside the curtain of the holy place was the "Altar of Burnt-Offerings" ('mizbaḥ ha-ʿolah'). This altar also became known as the Brazen Altar, or Altar of Bronze, because it was overlaid with that metal. It was there that the people brought the various offerings that they presented to Gods including the offering for sin. It was also upon this altar that the evening and the morning sacrifice were offered every day.

The terminology קֹדֶשׁ הַקֳּדָשִׁים ('qodesh haqodashem') is defined by the most sacred and forbidden inner chamber where God dwells. It was into the Holy of Holies where God's presence was manifested and God Himself

137 (Ex 25:17)

would visit.[138] Only the High Priest could come into this chamber once a year with a special blood-offering. It was from the 'qodesh haqodashem' that the word of the Lord would come, and it was the place designated as His throne room.

There were other things that were also referred to as 'qodesh haqodashem.' The priests were to eat the sacrifices in a place that was 'qodesh haqodashem,' which was probably before the 'parokhet' (veil of the Holy of Holies).[139] The offerings that they were to eat were also 'qodesh haqodashem.'[140] The Sin-Offering and the Trespass-Offering were 'qodesh haqodashem.'[141] However, any Sin-Offering whose blood was brought into the Tabernacle to make 'kapper' ("reconciliation") could not be eaten – it had become more sacred than all other offerings. It was 'qodesh haqodashem,' like the innermost chamber was 'qodesh haqodashem,' and was forbidden even to the priest. It was too holy for the priest to partake of and had to be burned with fire.[142] The bread of His presence was to be eaten by the priest every sabbath, which was 'qodesh haqodashem.'[143] The Brazen Altar was also referred to as 'qodesh haqodashem.'[144] The anointing

[138] (Ac 7:49; 17:24)
[139] (Num 18:7, 10)
[140] (Lev 2:3, 10; 6:17; 10:17)
[141] (Lev 6:25; 7:1; 14:13)
[142] (Lev 6:30)
[143] (Lev 24:8)
[144] (Ex 30:29; 40:10)

oil was called 'qodesh haqodashem.'[145] Anything devoted to the LORD was also 'qodesh haqodashem.'[146] During the future days of the Temple described by the prophet Ezekiel, the whole Temple and all the land assigned to the priest will be 'qodesh haqodashem.'[147] Even more today because we are the temple of the Holy Spirit we are qodesh haqodashem for God dwells in us.[148]

---

145 (Ex 30:36)
146 (Lev 28:8)
147 (Ezek 45:3; 48:12)
148 (Jn 14:17-23; 1 Cor 3:16)

Yom Kippur

"And the LORD has laid on Him the iniquity of us all."

-Isaiah 53:6c

Jesus became our Sin-Offering when He bore our sins in His own body on the cross. The cross that Jesus bled and died on became the greatest altar ever built to redeem men.[149] It was there, on the cross, that He ratified the New Covenant with His own blood. His blood became the means by which our sins are washed away.[150] Through the shedding of His blood, we were purged (καθαρισμός, 'katharismos') from our sins.[151] The final part of our redemption occurred when Jesus took His own blood and entered into the Holy of Holies. There, He purified (καθαρίζω) the heavenlies with His own blood.[152] When Jesus cleansed the heavenlies with His own blood, He

---

149 (2 Pet 2:24; Heb 13:10-14)
150 (Rev 1:5)
151 (Heb 1:3; 2 Pet 1:9; Heb 9:22; 1 Jn 1:9)
152 (Heb 9:23-24; cr Heb 8:5)

fulfilled what Yom Kippur testified of for more than 1,400 years. His blood remains forever effective to cleanse men from their sins – therefore, there is no need for another sacrifice.[153]

Yom Kippur was the one day out of the year that the High Priest was allowed to enter the Holy of Holies. The Holy of Holies was the place where God would come and dwell between the cherubim. Just as when Mount Sinai was set on fire with the presence of the LORD and was forbidden to all, even so the Holy of Holies was a place completely off-limits to man. The only One who can give men holiness made one man holy enough to come into the Holiest place on Earth to stand before the Holy God to make intercession for the holy people of Israel.

The altar inside the Holy of Holies was the "mercy seat" ('kapporet'), the most important and sacred of all Israel's altars and sacred objects. On the day of Yom Kippur, there were two goats that were chosen: one to purify the Holy of Holies (the goat for the LORD and one to carry away the sins of Israel (the goat for Azazel). The goat for the LORD was killed and then its blood was taken into the Holy of Holies to purify it from all of the rebellion and transgression of Israel.[154] The living goat would then carry Israel's sin away to Azazel into a desolate place – to a place-cut off – so that the goat would not be able to return

---

153 (Heb 10:14)
154 (Lev 16:16, 33)

again. It was through this that the testimony was given of the sins of Israel being purged from the Holy of Holies and sent away from their midst. The most important fact was that their sins had contaminated the throne of God and the blood of Yom Kippur removed them. This fact was underscored by the rabbis,

> "For pollution that befalls the Temple and its sancta through wantonness, kippur is made by the goat whose blood is sprinkled within the Holy Place and by the Yom Kippur". (m.Sebu 1:6; cf. Sipra, Ahare 5:8)

It was those sins that the "Yom Kippur" carried away into the wilderness.

It is certain that Jesus cleansed the Holy of Holies in Heaven with His own blood just as the earthly tabernacle was cleansed on Yom Kippur by the blood of animals.[155]

> *"It was therefore necessary that the patterns of things in the Heavens should be purified with these; but the heavenly things themselves with better sacrifices than these. For Christ is not entered into the holy places made with hands, which are the figures of the true, but into Heaven itself, now to appear in the presence of God for us:"*
>
> -Hebrews 9:11-12; 23–24

155 (Heb 6:19-20; 9:11-12, 23-24; 10:19-22)

As the Lamb of Passover, He ransomed us from sin and death. As the Lamb of the Sin-Offering, He cleansed us from our sins. As the goat for Azazel, He lifted them off of us and carried them away. As our Yom Kippur offering, He cleansed the heavenly realm and carried His blood into the Holy of Holies, the throne room of God in Heaven.

He was the Sin-Offering, the Trespass-Offering, and the Yom Kippur Offering. When He was slain, His blood purified every person who would believe. It rendered them absolutely holy so they could enter into the Holy of Holies.[156] Therefore the veil that separated the Holy of Holies was torn from top to bottom, showing that the way into the Holy of Holies was accessible to all by the blood of Jesus.[157] Christ Jesus was the Yom Kippur Offering to cleanse the heavenlies with His own blood.[158] He carried away all of the sins of our past as the goat carried away the sins of the nation of Israel that had contaminated His dwelling place.[159]

Christ Jesus was made the Sin-Offering for us to cleanse us from all our sins and His blood remains forever effective to cleanse us from sin.[160] Now Jesus forever remains the offering for sin. There is no longer any need

---

156 (Heb 10:19-22)
157 (Lk 23:45; Heb 9:8)
158 (Heb 9:23)
159 (1 Pet 2:24; Lev 16:21-23)
160 (Jn 1:29; 2 Cor 5:21; Rom 3:25)

for another sacrifice.[161] His blood is always available to cleanse us from our sins if we acknowledge them and forsake them.[162] There are those who would attempt to make the blood of Jesus effective for all – regardless if they believe – based on a misapplication of 1 John 2:2. However, His blood is only applicable for the sins of the whole world on the basis of a person walking in the light just as He is in the light.[163] When we walk in the light as Jesus is in the light, we have union with all those who are redeemed, and the blood of Jesus cleanses us from all sin. If we confess our sins, He is faithful and righteous to cleanse us from all sin. If we sin, He is our High Priest who makes Intercession to the Father. Jesus is the only One who can purify us, the only One who can remove our sins.

---

[161] (Heb 10:12, 14)
[162] (1 Jn 1:7, 9; Ps 32:5; Prov 28:13)
[163] (1 Jn 1:7)

The Divine Cleansing Agent

"For on that day shall the priest make a purgation for you, to cleanse you, that you may be clean from all your sins before the LORD."

-Leviticus 16:30

God will not abide in a polluted sanctuary, and the sins of Israel polluted His dwelling place. Therefore, there had to be a means of removing the contamination of sin.

> "All sin destroys fellowship with God. Cleansing from sin is denoted by כִּפֶּר (kipper)..." (Friedrich Büchsel and Johannes Herrmann, 1964).

The blood that was taken into the Holy of Holies was the divine cleansing agent used to remove the sin and decontaminate or purify the dwelling place of God. If the dwelling place was not purified, or if the contamination was beyond what the LORD could tolerate, then the result would be as described by the prophet Ezekiel,

> *"Surely because you have* ***polluted My sanctuary*** *with all your detestable things and with all your abominations, therefore I will cut you down; My eye will not spare, and I will not have pity."*
>
> -Ezekiel 5:11

Many of the words that we have chosen to describe what God did for the people of Israel fall short of their Hebrew counterparts. We must both be careful with the words that we use and the meanings that we ascribe to them. The word "atonement," for example, is a relatively new word that traces its origin to the 16th century, when it appeared as three separate words: "at-one-ment." While "at-one-ment" may speak of the restoration of relationship with God and the removal of the sin that stood between the worshipper and God, we question if it truly captures the full meaning of the Hebrew word or the Greek word that translates it in the LXX. Although the word "atonement" is used by the KJV many times in the Old Testament, it is only used one time in the New Testament.

Many scholars have used "atonement" to translate the Hebrew words 'kipper' and 'kippur,' but we must be careful that our usage does not dilute the meaning associated with these words. The KJV translated καταλλαγή ('katallage') as "atonement" in Romans 5:11. However, the closest Greek words for 'kipper' that are used in the New Testament are the words 'hilaskomai' and 'hilasmos.' Once again, we are faced with the challenge of translation. If we translate 'kipper' – or the Greek equivalent used in the LXX and New Testament: 'hilaskomai' or 'hilasmos' – as "expiation" or "propitiation," we may find ourselves actually changing the intended meaning.

> "Until recently it was widely held among evangelical and non-evangelical scholars alike that the term was related to an Arabic cognate with the meaning 'to cover.' This connection with the Arabic language has been virtually abandoned in modern scholarship. The interpretation of kipper as "cover" on the basis of Arabic, most recently supported by Stamm, is fraught with problems" (B. Lang, 1995).

There has been a failure to demonstrate this meaning in the Hebrew language as well as the methodological problem of using only Arabic to validate a Hebrew meaning. Thus, two other possibilities have been suggested. The first is to understand the verb as "to wipe" or "to purge." Support for this position comes from the fact that the cognate term in the Akkadian language had this meaning, and the verb occurs in parallelism to other Hebrew verbs within this semantic range.[164] This meaning works especially well when inanimate objects are the object of the verbal action. Another proposal is one that

---

[164] (Isa 27:9; Jer 18:21)

understands 'kipper' as a denominative verb from the noun 'kper,' which means "to ransom" (e.g., Ex 21:30). The idea would be that a person is paying a ransom for himself when he offers a sacrifice – Leviticus 17:11 provides a good illustration of this usage. The strongest evidence is the scripture itself, which describes the cultic ritual as a cleansing,[165] thus making טהר ('tihar,' "to cleanse") a synonym of 'kipper.' The whole process of the day of 'kippur' or 'kippurim' was to purify and cleanse the altar from the uncleanness caused by the sins of Israel. The result of 'kipper' for the altar was to reconcile ('kapper') it to God. Once something is cleansed then it is reconciled to God. This has far more descriptive and theological meaning than just to think of an atonement.

> *"And he shall go out unto the altar that is before the LORD, and make a reconciliation ('kapper') for it; and shall take of the blood of the bullock, and of the blood of the goat, and put it upon the horns of the altar round about. And he shall sprinkle of the blood upon it with his finger seven times, and cleanse ('tihar') it, and hallow ('qides,' "make holy") it from the uncleanness of the children of Israel. "...And when he has made an end of reconciling ('kapper') the holy place, the tabernacle of the congregation, and the altar..."*
>
> -Leviticus 16:18-20

165 (Lev 15:30-31; 16:19; Num 19:13, 20; cf. Jer 17:1)

The blood was in effect a divine cleaning agent, a fact that is actually born out in an etymological study of the Hebrew word 'kipper.'

> "In biblical poetry, 'kipper' is a synonym for 'macha' ("to wipe") (Jer 18:23) and 'hesir' ("to remove") (Isa 27:9) which suggests that 'kipper' means "to purge"'" (Jacob Milgrom, 2008; B. Lang, 1995).

In Ezekiel 43:20 and 26, it is used as a synonym for 'tihar' ("cleanse" or "purify") and 'chitte' ("decontaminate").[166] Additionally, the Akkadian word 'kuppuru,' whose Hebrew equivalent is 'kipper,' means "to rub" or "to wipe off," both referring to the act of cleaning an object. Even though the common translation for 'kipper' is "to atone" or "to expiate," there is much evidence that 'kipper' in many cases means "to purify" instead. It would have been essential that the cover of the Ark (Mercy Seat) – which had been contaminated by the pollution, rebellion, and sins of Israel – be purified so that it could remain as the dwelling place of the LORD in the midst of Israel.[167] It is of the utmost importance that the dwelling place of the LORD be pure and undefiled. Therefore, to understand the act of 'kipper' as removing the contamination is essential to the purpose of this sacrifice. If one views this as an expiatory role, then the effect of removing the sin is

---

[166] (Jer 18:23; Isa 27:9; Lev 14:48, 52, 58)
[167] (Lev 16:16)

compromised by virtue of the meaning of "to expiate," which is to nullify the effects of sin or to "cover it over." Certainly, the idea of covering sins is almost opposite to the removal of it. Such an idea may express deferment of the wrath of God, but the sin would remain. This cannot be the intended meaning of removing the sin that contaminated God's dwelling place, the Holy of Holies. How can that which is Holy of Holies remain so if it is contaminated with sin? Once there is sin, it is no longer holy, much less Holy of Holies!

Summary of the Words described above for kipper.

Hebrew	Transliteration	English
כִּפֶּר	kipper	atone/cleanse
כִּפֻּרִים	kippurim (pl)	atonements/ purgations
כִּפֻּר	kippur (sig)	atonement/ purgation
כַּפֹּר	kapper	reconciliation

At the very heart of the meaning of 'kipper' in Leviticus is the necessity for something to die and shed its blood to eliminate the contamination of sin. The sin that would prevent God from dwelling in the midst of His people had to be cleansed. The wages of sin is death and the laws of God cannot be broken. Therefore something had to die to pay the just penalty for sin. The death of the representative offering paid the price for sin and thus removed the sin. Therefore, the use of the word "expiate" is inappropriate to capture the meaning of 'kipper' or 'kippur.' Why? Because the sin was not covered but removed by the death of the offering. Furthermore, we learn from the New Testament that the sacrifice of Yom Kippur represented the blood of the Messiah used to purify (καθαρίζω, 'katharizo') the heavenly things. As is the type, so much more is the antitype.[168] Christ Jesus did not cover over the sin that contaminated the heavenly tabernacle He removed it. This not only adds support to the meaning proposed for the word 'kipper' and 'kippur,' but also causes us to realize that this is all about a sacrifice that God made for man and not one that man made for himself.[169] It would be totally wrong to think that God made an offering to nullify the way that sin affects His own person, He will have no interaction with it! Also, it is totally wrong to apply the concept of needing to appease God! God was already favorably disposed toward His

---

168 (Heb 6:19-20; 9:23-24; 10:19-22)
169 (1 Pet 2:24; Rev 1:5)

people. He is the God of love who loves humanity – He does not need appeasement!

Another common way that 'kipper' is translated is "to propitiate." It is the association of propitiation with atonement that further removes the meaning of atonement further away from cleansing. "Propitiate," like "atone," is somewhat of an abstract word. "Propitiate" refers to an appeasement, a covering, a turning away of wrath, a rubbing, or being ransomed through the action of a payment[170] through intercession,[171] or a representative/reconciler.[172] However, God does not need to be appeased – He reaches out to man rather than waiting for man to reach out to Him. This is not the intended meaning of the action of kipper.

We have additional support to the meaning of 'kipper' and 'kippur' by the way their Greek equivalents are used in the New Testament. In Romans 3:25, the Greek word 'hilasterion' is used to describe who Jesus is as our Redeemer. Our Redeemer's blood washed away our sins He did not cover them over. Our sins were so radically removed that we are referred to as a new creation.[173] They were so permanently removed that they are as far as the east is from the west.[174] The meaning of hilasterion cannot

170 (Ex 30:12-16; Num 1:53)
171 (Ex 32:30-34)
172 (Lev 16:21-22; 2 Cor 5:18-21)
173 (2 Cor 5:17)
174 (Heb 10:17; Ps 103:12; Jer 31:34)

be captured by the word 'propitiation.' Hilasterion was appropriately translated as "Mercy Seat" in Hebrews 9:5 by the KJV. 'Hilasterion' is the Greek word that translates the Hebrew word כַּפֹּרֶת ('kapporet'), which is the word for "Mercy Seat." This is evidenced by those who translated the Old Testament into Greek in the 2nd century BC – ἱλαστήριον ('hilasterion') translated the Hebrew word 'kapporet' (Mercy Seat).

Paul uses 'hilasterion' in Romans 3:25 to describe who Jesus is to us now,

> *"Whom God set forth as a ('hilasterion') "Mercy Seat" through faith in His blood, to reveal His righteousness by the passing over of the sins that had before taken place."*
>
> -Romans 3:25

The mercy seat represented that place where God dwells. The sins of the people were laid before the presence of God at the mercy seat where His feet rested. It was at the mercy seat that the blood could be applied to remove the sins that appeared before the presence of the LORD. As all the unrepented sins of Israel were laid upon the mercy seat and it was there that the blood was applied to remove those sins.[175] Jesus came as God manifested in the flesh, the very dwelling place of the Almighty, in a sacrificial

---

175 (Lev 16:16)

body.[176] God laid upon Him the sins of us all and He cleanse us from all of our sins with His own blood. Once again, we know that Jesus both purified καθαρίζω ('katharizo') us and also the Heavens with His own blood.[177] He did not cover over our sins but removed them! The word hilasteron is at the very center of the types and rituals that foreshadowed our deliverance from sin and cleaning by the blood of God. Hilasterion and its cognates are unmistakable connected with 'kapporet,' 'kapper,' 'kipper,' and 'katharizo' – all referring to the cleansing of those things belonging to the Tabernacle of the LORD and especially His throne room (the Holy of Holies).

'Hilasterion' ("Mercy Seat") and its cognates are used to describe both the process of cleansing from sin and its results. 'Hilasmos,' which is one of the cognates of 'hilasterion,' was also used by the Greeks to refer to the means by which men would appease the gods and avoid their wrath – and for this, the word "propitiation" was applied. However, the way that the Greeks used a word in their idolatrous practices should not be the basis of understanding these biblical Hebrew words. 'Hilasmos' is used in 1 John 4:10, which was also translated as "propitiation" in the KJV. We argue that such a concept should not be applied to the True and Living God! Rather,

---

176 (Heb 10:5,10)
177 (Heb 6:19-20; 9:23-24; 10:19-22)

it should be translated in line with 'kipper' or 'kippur' as something that purges or cleanses our sins. Once again, God did not need to be appeased like the gods of the Greeks. In His love, He gave us His only begotten Son to redeem us, to which all of these sacrifices testified.[178]

Therefore, the pagan Greek notion of propitiation or appeasement simply does not work! The redemption that is in Christ Jesus has nothing to do with the offerings or actions of men – much less their attempts to gain God's favor. It was God who offered up the sacrifice for us and freely gave us His favor. The secular world does not know of such a concept – therefore, they try to apply the ideas associated with false gods to the only true God. The message of salvation reaches far beyond the imagination and ideologies of men and their concepts of "god." Thus to limit God's actions by the words and definitions that men ascribe to them are misleading. We must understand the meanings of these words not only on the basis of linguistic research, but much more in view of what Jesus actually accomplished for us, which all these sacrifices and offerings witnessed for over 1,400 years.

We must use great caution in attempting to narrowly confine these New Testament Greek words to the meanings given in the secular and profane world. Equally, we must also recognize that at times there may have not been a perfect equivalent of the Hebrew word in the Greek

---

[178] (Jn 3:16; Rom 5:8; Eph 2:4-5)

vocabulary. For this reason, the antitype, Christ Jesus, and the context in which these words appear must guide us. Once again, when it comes to kipper and the ritual of dealing with those sins that contaminated the Holy of Holies the context demands the removal of those sins. The Holy of Holies had to be cleansed! Therefore, when we discover a definition that may not be primary to a word, but is in keeping with the Biblical evidence, we must give that meaning preeminence. We find such a definition for the word 'hilasmos': "purging," or "cleansing." When we choose to translate a word, it should be in agreement with what is implied by the context. We can be certain of what John meant by using 'hilasmos' in application to what Jesus did for us. For John taught that:

1. Our sins would be destroyed.[179]
2. The works of the Devil would be destroyed.[180]
3. We would receive cleansing from all of our sins.[181]
4. Christ Jesus would dwell in us, even as God dwelt in the Holy of Holies after it was purified.[182]
5. We would be born of God (complete and radical change).[183]

---

179 (1 Jn 3:5)
180 (1 Jn 3:8)
181 (1 Jn 1:7, 9; Rev 1:5)
182 (1 Jn 3:24; 4:4, 12, 15; 14:17-23; 15:1-7; 16:12-15; 17:21-23)
183 (1 Jn 3:9; 4:7; Jn 1:16; 3:1-6; 4:14; 7:37-39; etc..)

6. It would result in eternal life that we could now possess, thus referring to the quality of life that we received by the indwelling of the Holy Spirit.[184]

7. The cleansing gave us boldness before the judgment seat of God.[185]

8. If Christians do sin, they must look again to Jesus, who is the Intercessor who provides the 'hilasmos' ("forgiveness," "cleansing," or "purifying").[186]

The Apostle John used ἱλασμός ('hilasmos') twice in his first epistle (1 Jn 2:2; 4:10). In both instances, it was translated by the KJV as "propitiation." Yet, the Septuagint uses this same word to translate 'kippurim' in Leviticus 25:9 and Numbers 5:8. In Numbers 5:8, both ἱλασμοῦ ('hilasmos') and its cognate ἐξιλάσεται ('exilasetai') are found. 'Hilasmos' translates 'kippurim,' and 'exilasetai' translates 'kapper' ("to reconcile"). If we simply take the verse in the KJV and insert the word 'kippurim' where "propitiation" is found, we should immediately observe a different meaning. 'Kippurim' was the event when God removed the sins and rebellion of Israel from His midst. We should at least argue for "the removal of sin" or as we said previously "cleansing" or "purification." As a result,

[184] (1 Jn 1:2; 2:25; 3:15; 5:11, 13, 20)
[185] (1 Jn 2:28, 4:17)
[186] (1 Jn 1:7, 9; 2:2)

the verse would read, "And He is the 'Kippurim' ("cleansing" or "purification") for our sins…"[187]

The Hebrew word כִּפֵּר ('kipper'), (commonly translated as "atonement") is found 44 times in Leviticus. In total, "atonement" translates 'kipper' 83 times out of 100 in the KJV.[188] 'Kipper' is translated every time in the Septuagint (2nd Century B.C.) by ἐξιλάσκομαι ('exilaskomai'). The Greek word ἐξιλάσκομαι ('exilaskomai') is not used in the New Testament. The New Testament Greek word that is used in place of ἐξιλάσκομαι ('exilaskomai'), which would translate 'kipper,' is 'hilaskomai.' We have already mentioned two related cognates to this word: 'hilasmos' and 'hilasterion,' which are used two times each in the New Testament.[189] 'Hilasmos' also translates the plural noun 'kippurim.'[190] It also is found as a substitute word for 'exilaskomai' in Numbers 25:9, "the ram of 'kipper' ('hilasmos'), whereby 'kipper' ('exilaskomai') shall be made" (Friedrich Büchsel and Johannes Herrmann, 1964). All of these Greek words share the same root and are related to the idea of mercy. The noun ἱλασμός ('hilasmos') refers to a means of purgation/cleansing, ἱλαστήριον ('hilasterion') often refers to the Mercy Seat and the purifying sacrifice, and ἱλάσκομαι ('hilaskomai') is the verb "to make purgation." All of these Greek words are

---

187 (1 Jn 2:2)
188 (Friedrich Büchsel and Johannes Herrmann, 1964)
189 (1 Jn 2:2; 4:10; Rom 3:25; Heb 9:5)
190 (Lev 25:9)

cognates, all connected in meaning and usage, and they all contribute to that broader theme of God's merciful remedy to grant forgiveness by the removal of sin.

Greek	Transliteration	Hebrew/English
ἵλεως,	hileos	merciful/forgive
Ἱλάσκομαι ~ ἐξιλάσκομαι	hilaskomai exilaskomai	kipper/ mercy purify/atonement
ἱλασμός,	hilasmos	kipper & kippurim/ purify/atonement
ἱλαστήριον	hilasterion	kapporet/ Mercy Seat

The first time that 'kipper' is found, it is translated by the Greek word 'exilaskomai' in Genesis 32:21. In this context, Jacob is sending presents to his brother, Esau, to honor him, and to let him know that he is submitting all he has to his brother's authority. The first time that the verb כָּפַרְתָּ ('kafar-ta') and the noun כֹּפֶר ('koper') are used – which share the same root with 'kipper' – is in

Genesis 6:14. It is commonly translated as “to cover” or “to pitch.” However, we could equally translate it as “to smear” (כָּפַר, ‘kafar’) as in “smear it within and without with asphalt” (כֹּפֶר, ‘koper,’ “oil sludge”).[191] There is certainly no strong argument that this context defines the meaning of this cognate of ‘kipper’ as “to cover.”

Jesus did not come to “cover over” sin – He appeared for the purpose of taking away the sin of the world and destroying the works of the Devil.[192] He cleanses (καθαρίζει, ‘katharizei’) us of our sins, and is thus the Purifier, not the propitiation.[193] When Paul uses this word in connection with what Jesus did for us, we must understand that he is referring to the removal of the sin – just as the sins were wiped away (‘kippur’) when they were removed from the altar on Yom Kippur. It was the sins of the past that were removed on Yom Kippur, not the sins of the future. Once the sin was removed on Yom Kippur, it was clean only until the rebellion and the iniquity of sin contaminated it again.

God did not execute judgement against us because of our sins, but instead He sent His only begotten Son to be the Lamb and Sacrifice for our sins.[194] All of our sins were laid upon His body, even as they were laid upon the goat that was sent away, which was never to return. Just as the

---

191 (Gen 6:14)
192 (Jn 1:29, 36; 1 Jn 3:5, 8; Rev 1:5; Heb 1:3; 1 Pet 2:24; Col 2:11)
193 (1 Jn 1:7, 9; 2:2)
194 (Rom 5:10; Col 1:21; Eph 2:2-3)

blood of the goat was chosen for the Lord and was applied to the Mercy Seat to remove the sins from the altar, the blood of Jesus wiped all of our sins away. We can also say that His blood wiped away our sins from the presence of God in Heaven where our sins stood as a testimony against us.[195] It was through His death that our sins were wiped away and the power of spiritual death removed from our lives.[196] It is so important to recognize that Jesus took away (ἀναφέρω, 'anaphero') the sin, which emphasizes its removal.[197] This helps us to further understand the meaning of 'kipper' and 'kippur.'

It is because of Jesus that all of the glory of God can come into our lives and remain.[198] Thus, Paul proclaimed Jesus to be the place where purgation for sin was accomplished.[199] Paul leaves no question as to how he viewed the 'hilasterion,' for he announces the removal of the sins of the past by Jesus Christ. Therefore, we should recognize 'kipper' and 'kippur' as the removal of the sin from God's altar. In one single word, Paul both equates Jesus to the altar and the activity of 'kippur': the removal of sin by His blood.

---

195 (Heb 8:5; 9:23-24; Lev 16:16)
196 (1 Pet 2:24; Rom 6:6)
197 (1 Pet 2:24)
198 (Jn 14:23; Lk 24:49; Jn 17:22)
199 (Rom 3:25; Lev 16:16)

Reconciliation

"For God was in Christ reconciling the world unto Himself, not counting their trespasses against them, and has committed unto us the word of reconciliation."

-2 Corinthians 5:19

The message of reconciliation is interwoven into the 'kippur' ritual. There are several places where the piel form of 'kippur' is translated as "reconcile."[200] The act of reconciliation produces the change, which is the result of the cleansing ritual as observed on Yom Kippur (The Day of Atonement). Any time the blood of a sacrifice is brought into the Tabernacle, it makes 'kapper' (reconciliation). Reconciliation should be understood as the restoration of holiness. The sacrifices of 'kippur' did just that – it removed the sin that contaminated the Holy of Holies.

---

200 (Lev 6:30; 16:20; Ezek 45:20)

The blood of these sacrifices that made 'kapper' (reconciliation) and was brought into the Tabernacle was the extreme of what is 'qodesh haqodashem' (Holy of Holies) and was forbidden for the priest to eat.[201] As we have been pointing out, Yom Kippur was a foreshadowing of what the Redeemer, Christ Jesus, would do for us when He came. When Jesus came, He brought complete reconciliation by removing the sin and its power and dominion over our lives. His blood would be the sacrifice for sins. Yet even more, His blood would remain efficacious if we should sin after being redeemed. There would be no need for another sacrifice, for His blood would be invoked for cleansing by confessing our sins.[202] Jesus made reconciliation with His own blood for the sins of anyone who would seek to be redeemed.[203]

The word "reconciliation" is translated from the Greek word ἱλάσκομαι ('hilaskomai'), which shares the same root ἵλεως ('ileos') and in the same family of those similar words highlighted previously: 'hilasmos' and 'hilasterion.' This family of Greek words translates the Hebrew 'kpr' family: 'kipper' (atonement, purify), 'kipporet' (propitiation, mercy seat), and 'kapper' (reconciliation).

> "The concepts of purification, cleansing, and consecration are all found in the ritual of the great

[201] (Lev 6:30)
[202] (1 Jn 1:7, 9; Ps 32:5; Prov 38:18; Rev 2:5, 16, 21-22; 3:3, 19)
[203] (Heb 2:17; 1 Jn 2:2)

Day of Atonement" (Friedrich Büchsel and Johannes Herrmann, 1964).

The result of this grace offered in the Old Testament provided a cleansing from sin until Christ Jesus came. The cleansing was focused more on the dwelling place of God, which the sins of the people contaminated, more than anything else. The cleansing that the people of Israel received would be on the basis of faith in the coming Redeemer.[204]

However, knowing that the blood of bulls and goats could never take away sin from the heart of man, there is a new kind of reconciliation in the New Testament. New Testament reconciliation brings those who trust in the blood of Jesus to the redemption that only God's blood can supply. It has thoroughly washed us from our sins and brought forth a new heart and a new spirit. The blood of Jesus completely removes the sins of the past and delivers us from the law of sin and death.[205] Now, reconciliation is understood in terms of a new creation that has been made one with God. Reconciliation takes on the full meaning that Yom Kippur, or the Day of Atonement, could only foreshadow. Reconciliation is a complete change that has taken place by the exchange of the life of Christ Jesus for our own life.

---

[204] (Job 19:25; Jn 8:56; Heb 11:13; 1 Pet 1:11-12)
[205] (Rom 3:25; 8:1-3; Rev 1:5; 7:14; 2 Cor 5:21; 1 Jn 1:9)

The word "reconcile" in Romans 5:11 is from the Greek word 'katallage.' In Romans, the translators of the Authorized Version rendered it as "atonement," thus recognizing the relationship between reconciliation and atonement, or 'kapper' and 'kattalage.' Even though the Greek word that most commonly translates 'kippur' is 'ἐξιλάσκομαι' ("exilaskomai"), the translators of the KJV recognized the relationship that exists between 'kippur' and "reconcile" as observed in Leviticus 6:30, 16:20, and Ezekiel 45:20, where 'kapper' in the Hebrew and 'exilaskomai' in Greek (LXX) were translated as "reconcile." Thus, we may say that 'kippur,' just like 'kapper,' carries the meaning "to reconcile."

The one word used more than any other in the New Testament for reconciliation is καταλλάσσω, 'katallasso.' It has the same root as καταλλαγή 'katallage,' which is translated as "atonement" in Romans 5:11. These words are used interchangeably in Romans 5:10-11 and 2 Corinthians 5:18-20.

> "In fact, the earlier meaning of the English word "atonement" was 'the reconciliation of two estranged parties'" (Robert Jamieson, A. R. Fausset, and David Brown, 1997).

Also Robinson's word-study points out concerning Romans 5:11 that, "Atonement, properly, reconciliation, the noun being etymologically akin to the verb to reconcile. Atonement at the time of the A. V. signified reconciliation, at-one-ment, the making of two estranged parties at one." (Marvin Richardson Vincent, 1887). It is insightful to note that 'katallasso' can be understood as "to change by exchange."

> "In 2 C. 5:18 it is introduced as the basis of the most comprehensive renewal possible for man, namely, that he has become a new creature, that old things have passed away and that all things have become new. In R. 5:10, too, it denotes an incisive change" (Friedrich Büchsel, 1964).

To be reconciled is to be changed by an exchange. Christ Jesus changed us by exchanging His life for ours. He took all of our sins upon Himself as the sin offering, and in doing so He made us the righteousness of God in Him.[206] Now we are cut off from sin and are empowered to live unto righteousness.[207] This is the exchange: Christ Jesus gave His life for us so that we might receive His life as our own. Through this, we are able to understand that reconciliation is indeed parallel to justification, for we are made a new creation by the reconciliation. Much more than just the removal of guilt is witnessed in reconciliation, for that which is old has passed away, and the new has come.[208] At the heart of the message of

[206] (2 Cor 5:21)
[207] (2 Pet 2:24)
[208] (1 Cor 5:17)

salvation is, "You must be born again," and "If any man is in Christ, he is a new creation." In this we find the true definition of reconciliation and the meaning of "be reconciled to God."[209]

Reconciliation, like justification, speaks of the great mystery of redemption in which we were spiritually crucified with Christ. Even as we were crucified together with Him, we were also raised up together with Him. Now we are alive together with Him and seated in Heaven together with Him. We can now say that the life of Christ Jesus even extends beyond a "representative offering," for we were spiritually crucified together with Him.[210] This is far-removed from any concept of a "substitutionary offering" or "vicarious offering," for the reconciliation has made us together with Him in death, resurrection, life, and glorification. Now, He lives in us, and we live in Him and have been made partakers of His life – this is the reconciliation. Through the new birth, we were recreated in righteousness and true holiness to live as one with God – this is the reconciliation. As He was our representative in life and death, in the resurrection and glorification we may now be His representatives on the Earth. New Testament reconciliation is the greatest expression of change known to Scripture, for we no longer

---

[209] (2 Cor 5:20)
[210] (Gal 2:20; 6:14; Rom 6:6)

live – Christ Jesus has imparted His life into us, and for us to live is Christ.

Hebrew	Transliteration	Greek	Transliteration	English
כַּפֵּר	kapper	ἐξιλάσκομαι	exhilaskomai	Reconcile
		Ἱλάσκομαι	hilaskomai	Reconciliation
		καταλλαγή	katallage	Reconciliation
		καταλλάσσω	katallasso	Reconcile

Confession Is Part of Cleansing

"If we should confess our sins, He is faithful and righteous to forgive us of the sins and to cleanse us from all unrighteousness."

-1 John 1:9

In order for the cleansing ritual to be complete, the goat that would bear the sins of the people on Yom Kippur had to be properly handled.[211] After the ritual was complete for the goat that was used to cleanse the temple, the next step was to provide a means to send away the sins of the people. In order for their sins to be dealt with, the high priest had to lay his hands on the goat and confess all of the iniquities of Israel –thereby putting them on the head of the goat.[212] The sins were conveyed to the goat by confession.

"And Aaron shall lay both his hands upon the head of the live goat and confess over him all the iniquities of

211 (Lev 16:10)
212 (Lev 16:21, 30)

the children of Israel, and all their transgressions in all their sins, putting them upon the head of the goat..."

-Leviticus 16:21

Forgiveness for sins was not granted until the entire ritual was complete. "For on that day shall the priest make reconciliation ('kapper') for you, to cleanse (טהר', 'taher') you, that you may be clean (טהר', 'taher') from all your sins before the LORD."[213] Keep in mind that this was a cleansing for the *Tabernacle*. It was not possible that the blood of bulls and goats could take away sin.[214] The sins of the people were purified only with respect to being removed from the presence of the LORD in the Tabernacle. They were also removed from the people with respect to them being carried away by the goat to Azazel.

The burnt offering that was brought to the door of the Tabernacle called for the offerer to lay his hand upon its head.[215] There was nothing said about confession or the transference of sin. However, we know it was the act of designation for the offerer, thus becoming the representation of the offerer. The same is true when Aaron and his sons laid their hands upon the sin offering, which was then designated to purify their sins.[216] It is safe to assume that whether the hand-leaning rite described the

213 (Lev 16:30, cr. Ps 51:2)
214 (Heb 11:4)
215 (Lev 1:4)
216 (Lev 8:14; Ex 29:10)

transference of sins or not, it was indeed a transference, for in Christ Jesus God laid upon Him the sins of us all.[217] The hand-leaning rite was witnessed by most of the animal offerings: Peace-Offering, Sin-Offering, and Yom Kippur Offering.[218] However, for those animal offerings that did not mention the hand-leaning rite, the sacrificial act by itself can be understood as confession enough, because they are acknowledging their sin by offering a sacrifice for their sins. When the offerer laid his hand upon the sacrifice, the offering was designated as that which represented his own life. However, on the Yom Kippur, the transference of the sins was made even more evident. Both hands were laid upon the sacrifice, and a confession was made, which then resulted in the sins being transferred to the goat. In a similar fashion, God laid upon Jesus Christ the sins of us all so that He could bear them away.[219] All of our sins are transferred to Jesus by confession.[220] After the confession of the sins and iniquities, the goat was led away into a "wilderness place" to one named Azazel. Israel was only able to rejoice in seeing their sins sent away. However, we rejoice in seeing our sins sent away by the death of Jesus and in our new life having begun in His resurrection from the dead.

---

[217] (Isa 53:6; 2 Pet 2:24; 2 Cor 5:21)
[218] (Lev 2:2; 4:4; 16:21)
[219] (Heb 9:26; 1 Pet 2:24)
[220] (Rom 10:9-10; 1 Jn 1:9; Rev 2:5; 2 Cor 12:21; Ac 17:30)

Confessing of sins was also witnessed in the Trespass-Offering, but there was no hand-leaning rite mentioned.[221] The Trespass-Offering required confession and restitution, but does not mention the hand leaning rite but does require confession. First, confession had to be made, then the restitution value had to be paid to the one trespassed against, then the blood of the ram could be offered to make atonement.[222] The prophet Jeremiah called for anyone who had sin to acknowledge their iniquities and that they would then find forgiveness with God.[223] God called out to Israel on many occasions to confess their sins and to turn from them with the invitation to be forgiven.[224] David cried out to the Lord to cleanse him from his sins on the basis that he acknowledged his sin, which would involve a confession of his sins.[225] However, in every case, we know that without the shedding of blood there is no forgiveness.[226]

In ancient times, Israel had the Mercy Seat where the blood was applied by the high priest. Today, we have the throne of grace that we approach. Each person may now come boldly before the presence of the Lord. The One who was tempted in every respect as we are tempted stands ready to make intercession for our sins and to

---

221 (Lev 5:5)
222 (Num 5:6-8)
223 (Jer 3:13)
224 (Lev 26:40; Ezra 10:11; Neh 9:2)
225 (Ps 51:3)
226 (Heb 9:22)

supply us with the mercy that we need.[227] Our Advocate and Intercessor, though He was sinless in His trial, is ready to help us in ours. He makes intercession for our sins as our High Priest and supplies us with the strength and ability to overcome all that we are faced with. He makes that intercession with His own blood. How much more then is the effectiveness of the intercession of our High Priest with His own blood than that of the Aaronic priesthood under the Law. Jesus remains the Mercy Seat for our sins – and not for ours only, but for the sins of the whole world. He purges our conscience from the works of sin so that we may serve the living God.[228] He is indeed the One who saves us to the uttermost, as His blood is always there to provide the cleansing that we may need.

> "All that we can need is comprehended in two things, "mercy and grace;" the one, for the pardon of our past transgressions; the other, for the preservation of our souls from sin in future" (Charles Simeon, 1833).

Today, the appropriation of the blood of Jesus that cleanses from all sin is still accompanied by acknowledging the sin and turning from it. Paul said that if we confess with our mouth and believe in our hearts that God raised Jesus from the dead, we will be saved. Confession is made

---

[227] (Heb 4:15-16)
[228] (Heb 9:13-14)

unto salvation...[229] It is at that moment that we confess with our mouth and believe in our hearts that we partake of what Jesus did for us 2,000 years ago. Our salvation and cleansing begins there and continues on from there. John said that if we walk in the light as He is in the light, then we have a fellowship (a union) one with another, and the blood of Jesus Christ cleanses us from all sin.[230] The present active indicative καθαρίζει ('katharizo') as found in 1 John 1:7 is the present tense verb that describes action right now: "...the blood of Jesus cleanses (καθαρίζει) us..." It is only ongoing in the futuristic sense by the active participation of confessing of any sins that are committed.[231] The blood of Jesus never loses its power to cleanse:

> *"If we confess our sins, He is faithful and righteous to cleanse us..." We should all learn how to properly parse Greek verbs and not make more of them than is presented in the context in which they are found. It is the blood of Christ Jesus that cleanses us, and if we sin, by a confession of those sins the blood goes on cleansing us."*
>
> -1 John 1:9

[229] (Rom 10:9-10)
[230] (1 Jn 1:7)
[231] (1 Jn 1:9)

Immediately connected with verse 7 is the promise that if we sin, we must confess our sins and He is faithful and righteous to cleanse us from our sin.[232]

Anyone who does not believe that you have to confess your sins and turn from them can only argue their point from a philosophy of redemption. They cannot prove their point from the Old Testament application of the blood, nor from purely dealing with all the scriptures on the subject in the New Testament. This is a dangerous theological game for people to play! There are no examples in Scripture that demonstrate that once something is cleansed that it cannot be contaminated again. The Holy of Holies was continually contaminated by the sins of Israel and had to be cleansed annually. The people themselves were continually contaminated by their sins, and as a result, they had to bring their sin-offerings and guilt-offerings to deal with them. It is repeated over and over again in Scripture that sin contaminates and corrupts a person. The issue becomes an almost ridiculous argument as to whether or not it's essential to acknowledge your sin and to ask for forgiveness. In any walk of life, if you do not acknowledge that you are doing something wrong, then you can never make the adjustment to do it correctly. To believe that you do not have to ask for forgiveness if you have wronged another person goes against every principle of relationship. It's just

[232] (1 Jn 1:9)

this simple: the blood was shown for more than 1,400 years to deal with sin only on the basis of those sins being recognized and confessed – then the blood became efficacious to make intercession. Today, Jesus' blood is applied for our sins on our behalf anytime we acknowledge those sins. Christ Jesus, as our High Priest, applies His blood that was shed 2,000 years ago and cleanses us from sin. If the type does not depict the antitype, then the type has no meaning.

Paul said that if we see a brother overtaken in a trespass, that those who are spiritual must seek to restore him.[233] James calls out the need to confess our trespasses one to another, which when applied properly means to confess to the one who was trespassed against when possible. He makes confession a prerequisite of being healed of the trespass.[234] Jesus also demanded us to leave our offering at the altar and to be reconciled to our brother if there was a transgression.[235] Furthermore, if we are to be forgiven, we have to forgive. Forgiveness always involves some kind of confession and release. The Lord Jesus places forgiving others at the highest order of responsibility. If we do not forgive others, then He will not forgive us.[236] If we are already forgiven of future sins and

---

233 (Gal 6:1)
234 (Jam 5:16)
235 (Mt 5:23-24; 18:15)
236 (Mt 6:11, 14-15; Lk 11:4)

have no need of seeking forgiveness, then these and many other scriptures have no meaning.

The Purgation Offering: Sin Eliminated

> *"Come now and let us reason together,' says the LORD: 'Though your sins be as scarlet, they shall be as white as snow; though they be red like crimson, they shall be as wool.'"*
>
> -Isaiah 1:18

The offering commonly known as the Sin-Offering was also used to purify the altars from the sins of the people. The Hebrew word for sin is חַטָּאת ('chattat'). This is one of the most frequently used words in the Bible. It is translated as "sin" in approximately 632 verses in the King James Bible. When the *offering* for sin is referred to in the Hebrew Bible, it is the same word that is translated as sin. The Sin-Offering, or 'chattat,' in its piel form, may also refer to being "purified" and can be rendered as the "Purgation-Offering." The Septuagint understood 'chattat' to mean "sin" and thus translated it consistently with the

Greek 'hamartia'. However, when we refer to 'chattat' as both "sin" and also "Sin-Offering," we are also referring to it as a purifying offering. Keep in mind that the sin of a person contaminated the dwelling place of the LORD which then had to be decontaminated. David said that when He sinned, He sinned against the LORD alone and did evil in His sight.[237] We know that David expected that the cleansing or the purifying would ultimately be extended to his life.[238] David asked to be washed from his sin, which he saw as being made so clean that there would be no stain of it remaining – he described it as "whiter than snow."[239] When the blood of God touches you no stain of sin remains.

As we have said, it was by the hand-leaning rite that a person was able to designate an offering for himself. The closest possibility to getting rid of sin was the impartation of his sin into the animal without blemish and the subsequent execution of that animal. When the representative offering was executed the sin was executed. Yet more importantly this offering for sin witnessed the shed blood of the coming Redeemer, Christ Jesus. The means to justly deal with sin was to execute the judgment against sin which was death. To give witness of the coming Redeemer there had to be one that could pay for the sin of another with its own life.

---

237 (Ps 51:4)
238 (Ps 51:2)
239 (Ps 51:7; cr Isa 1:18)

What we have attempted to emphasize was the removal of sin that stood between the worshipper and God. The sin had to be removed from before the presence of the LORD which is expressed in the cleansing of the altar by the blood. We must appreciate that the altar itself had been contaminated by the sins of the people, and therefore the blood needed to act as the agent of holiness that could remove the sin.[240] When the blood was placed upon the altar, God saw that the penalty for sin had been paid for by faith in the blood of the representative offering. Sin was removed out of the way between God and the worshipper, and it was no longer accounted to the person who offered the sacrifice.

We learn from Yom Kippur that nothing impure or unholy could come into the Holy of Holies. On Yom Kippur, only the high priest who had been made holy could enter. To enter, he had to bathe his entire body and then put on his holy garments. Then he had to be very cautious not to in any way make himself impure or unclean before coming in. Therefore, it would be all the more necessary that the blood that he had brought to cleanse the altar was also pure and holy, and therefore classified as most holy, 'qodesh haqodashem.'[241] We know that the hand-leaning rite and confession imparted the sins of Israel into the sacrifice. Therefore we can begin to

---

240 (Lev 16:16; Ezek 5:11; 2 Chron 23:29; Num 18:23)
241 (Ex 30:10)

see that the life of the innocent sacrifice for sin was able to nullify the effect of sin and yet remain pure. The blood of the pure sacrifice was therefore able to absorb the impurity of sin and still remain pure. Because God had made the provision for the blood to be used to provide 'kipper' ("cleansing"), the blood of the sacrifice swallowed up the death and impurity of sin, even as light swallows up darkness and death is swallowed up in victory.[242] The only thing that can purify that which has become impure is the pure and perfect sacrificial offering.

The pure being uncontaminated by the impure was demonstrated in the ministry of Jesus. He was able to touch the unclean person when it was forbidden for everyone else. When Jesus laid His hand on the unclean, they became clean while Jesus Himself remained clean.[243] The pure and holy Lamb of God was never contaminated by the uncleanness that surrounded Him. Furthermore, He was also able to take the sins of the whole world upon Himself and not be altered by the sin. Through His death, He destroyed the one who has the power of death – that is, the Devil.[244] He took our sins in His own body and remained the pure and holy Lamb of God.[245] He was able

[242] (1 Cor 15:54)
[243] (Mt 8:3; Mk 5:41)
[244] (Heb 2:14)
[245] (1 Pet 2:24; Jn 1:29)

to take our sins and give us His holiness, he took our uncleanness and gave us His purity.[246]

When Jesus purified us with His own blood as the Lamb of God, He was made the Sin-Offering, but sin did not contaminate Him or His blood.[247] He then entered into the Holy of Holies in Heaven and presented His blood – which is pure and holy – to purify the heavenly Holy of Holies. His blood remains the purifying agent that also purifies all those who would be made the temple of God unto this day and forevermore.[248] By His blood, He makes everyone pure and holy who put their trust in Him.[249]

---

246 (Col 1:22; 1 Pet 1:19)
247 (2 Cor 5:21)
248 (1 Cor 3:16; 6:19; 2 Cor 6:16; Heb 13:20)
249 (Heb 2:11; 10:10, 14)

Passover

"By faith he kept the Passover and the sprinkling of blood, lest the destroyer of the firstborn should touch them."

-Hebrews 11:28

There is nothing that demonstrates the power that ransomed us like the blood of the Passover. God promised Israel – on the night when He allowed the destroyer to execute his claims on those dwelling in Egypt – that if they would apply the blood of a lamb to their doorpost and lintel, they would be protected. The blood of the lamb would be the ransom payment to show that the death of the firstborn was paid in full. The Hebrew word for redeem is פָּדָה ('padah'), which describes the payment that must be paid to pay the redemption price. That night, God testified that the price of man's redemption was valued at the price of God's own life. That night, the lamb was offered as a ransom for the firstborn of every

household, and the applied blood was the proof.[250] The lamb that was offered was a spotless lamb without blemish. This testified of the purity and sinlessness of the coming Redeemer, Christ Jesus.

The blood applied to their houses distinguished them from all others. The redeeming blood identified them as those who belonged to God. The blood removed all claims of death and identified them as the ransomed of God. The blood of the lamb that was slain that night testified of the

250 (Ex 12:1-14; Deut 7:8; 13:5)

Lamb of God that was yet to come to purchase them and deliver all who would put their trust in Him. It was the blood of Jesus that would ἀγοράζω ('agorazo', "purchase") all who will put their trust in the coming Messiah.[251] We are those who are His purchased possession, bought with the price, and redeemed not with silver and gold, but by His precious blood.[252]

Also, nothing in the Old Testament more clearly demonstrates the delivering power of God than the Passover. It was at this time that God came and saved His people – He redeemed them unto Himself and delivered them from their slavery. It is in this story that the most fundamental concepts of salvation are captured. Salvation should not be a subjective or elusive term, because it is so clearly demonstrated for us by what God did for His people when He brought them up out of Egypt. When Israel was saved out of Egypt, they were not partially or progressively saved from the power of Pharaoh, but were completely removed from the dominion of Egypt and its forces. We should not wonder how saved and separated to God we are when we have such a witness of our salvation. He brought us out of the kingdom of this world into the Kingdom of His dear Son and made us His holy people.[253] Now we have the life of the One who gave His life for us. We are united with the One who paid the ransom price for

---

251 (Rev 5:9-10)
252 (Eph 1:14; 1 Cor 6:20; 7:23; 1 Pet 1:18)
253 (Ex 19:6; Lev 20:26; 1 Pet 1:16-16; 2:9; Jn 17:14,16; Col 1:13)

our salvation. Now we share with Him in all that He possesses.[254]

The Passover-Offering takes a central position in the New Testament. It was on the night before Passover that Jesus ate the Passover meal with the disciples. That night the Passover meal was commemorated as the communion table. The next day at the time of the slaying of the Passover lamb the true Passover Lamb was slain. Jesus became our Passover Lamb and poured out His blood so that we might be ransomed, redeemed, and liberated from Satan to become the people of God. The Passover Lamb brought forth a new heart and a new spirit through the new birth.[255]

The yearly Passover feast has now moved into a feast of a different kind: a celebration of the union between God and the redeemed. The elements of the feast basically remain the same, but instead of sacrificing and eating a lamb, we now take the bread of communion. The Bread of Life – which is the Word of God, the True Manna sent down from God – became our sacrifice. When we partake of the broken bread, we are partaking of His body.[256] The blood – which is the life of the flesh that had been forbidden – is now given to us to drink, because His life has become ours.[257] Even though it is only the fruit of the

---

[254] (Rom 8:17; Eph 2:6; Gal 4:7)
[255] (1 Cor 5:7; Ezek 36:25-26; Jn 3:5)
[256] (Mt 26:26; Jn 6:32, 35, 41, 48-51, 56)
[257] (Mt 26:27-28; 1 Cor 10:16; 11:25)

vine, it represents the blood of the sacrifice that was shed to ratify the New Covenant. Jesus said, "Unless you eat My flesh and drink My blood, you have no life in you," thus calling all men everywhere to come and partake of His sacrificial offering. If we will respond to the call of redemption, then He will dwell in us and we will dwell in Him.[258]

The Passover meal, which became the communion meal, most clearly represents the union that we now have with God in Christ Jesus. If we eat His flesh and drink His blood, then He dwells in us and we dwell in Him.[259] This communion or "common union" is represented as a branch in a vine.[260] This union is so immense that the Holy Spirit, the Father, and Christ Jesus have come to dwell in us.[261] Our union now is like the union that Jesus has with the Father.[262] Every time we partake of this New Testament Passover, we testify that we have been brought back into the family of God and that Christ Jesus dwells in us and we dwell in Him.[263]

On Passover, all of the leaven must be removed, which represents sin.[264] This is a testimony of our separation from all that is not of God. His blood purified us and

---

[258] (Jn 5:56)
[259] (Jn 6:56)
[260] (Jn 15:1-7)
[261] (Jn 14:17-23)
[262] (Jn 17:21-23)
[263] (1 Jn 3:24; 4:13, 15-16)
[264] (Ex 12:15,19; 1 Cor 5:7-8)

removed all of our sin. Now we are commanded to keep ourselves unspotted by the world. God demands that we purge out all of the leaven that would attempt to mix with our lives.[265] The purging out shares the same root as cleansing (καθαρος, 'katharos'), which finds a parallelism in Scripture with reconciliation.[266] Just as we are commanded not to have leaven with the Passover, even so every impurity of sin must be treated the same. He has purified our spirit, souls, and bodies with His blood, making us a tabernacle where God can dwell.We are then to keep ourselves pure and clean.[267] He has washed us from our sins, purified our heart, made us the righteousness of God, and empowered us to be holiness unto the Lord! Now we are commanded to purify ourselves from all of the uncleanness of spirit and flesh – we are to mortify every deed of our life.[268]

---

265 (1 Cor 5:6-8; Gal 5:9)
266 (1 Cor 5:8; 2 Cor 7:1; 1 Jn 3:3; Rom 8:13; Col 3:5)
267 (1 Thess 5:23; 1 Pet 1:22; Ac 15:9; 2 Cor 7:1; 1 Jn 3:3; Rom 8:13; Col 3:5; 1 Jn 5:18)
268 (2 Cor 7:1; Col 3:15; Rom 8:13)

Conclusion

"Whom God set forth as a Mercy Seat through faith in His blood, to reveal His righteousness by the passing over of the sins that had before taken place"

-Romans 3:25

When Jesus died for us at Calvary and offered His own blood to cleanse us from our sins, God tore open the veil that separated us from His presence and has invited all to come near.[269] Today, when we come to God we walk directly into the Holy of Holies. The Holy of Holies was not made less holy – rather, access was granted to all who were made holy by the blood of Jesus.[270] The earthly tabernacle was only a sketch and a figure of the true Holies of Holies in Heaven.[271] The Holies of Holies is the throne room of God.[272] When Jesus poured out His life for

---

[269] (Mt 27:51; Mk 15:38; Lk 23:45)
[270] (Heb 10:19-21)
[271] (Heb 8:5; 9:24; Ex 25:9, 40)
[272] (Ps 11:4; Hab 2:20; 2 Sam 6:2; 1 Chron 13:6; 1 Sam 4:4; Ps 99:11; Isa 37:16; Ezek 10:1-4; Heb 4:16; 8:1; 12:2; Rev 4:2-10; 5:1, 6, 13; 7:9-17; 8:3)

us, He was also providing the means by which His life would be poured into us. His death not only destroyed the power of Satan that dominated our lives, it also provided the means by which we would receive a new heart and a new spirit. His life was exchanged for ours- He took our sin and we received His righteousness. He took our uncleanness and we received His holiness. When His life was poured into us, His life destroyed the power of death held over us.[273] When we were born of the Spirit, we stepped into the life of Christ and the life of Christ stepped into us.[274]

---

[273] (Rom 8:2; 2 Cor 1:10)
[274] (Rom 8:1, 12:5; 1 Cor 1:30; 2 Cor 5:17; Eph 2:10; Col 1:27; Jn 14:23; 15:1; 1 Jn. 3:24; 4:13-16)

During the time of the first tabernacle, there was only one opportunity to enter into the Holies of Holies and that was during the yearly purification of Yom Kippur.[275] There was only one person who could enter into this most sacred realm, and that was the high priest. As the high priest he came with the only cleansing agent that had the power to remove the sin that contaminated the altar. He came with the power of the blood that made him holy and acceptable to God. He came with the power of the blood that would remove all the sins of Israel from before the presence of the LORD. On the Day of Kippur, the sin and its testimony against man was removed and the sins the people committed that year were sent away, never to return.[276]

All of those sacrifices and rituals of the Old Testament foreshadowed what could only be truly brought to pass in Christ Jesus. Through the blood of Jesus we have been given the holiness that allows us to live in the heavenly Holy of Holies. We are seated there together with Christ at the right hand of the Father.[277] We not only dwell with God but He dwells in us and has made our life His Holy dwelling place.[278] Through the blood of Christ Jesus, we live in union with the Almighty God. We are those who draw near unto God by the blood of the Lamb and live in the reality of what the first covenant could only typify.

---

275 (Lev 16:2)
276 (Lev 16:1-16)
277 (Eph 2:6; Rom 8:30)
278 (1 Cor 3:16; 6:19; 2 Cor 6:16)

God is not just pleased to dwell in our midst – He now dwells in us!

There is yet another dimension of this unseen interaction that we have with God in the Spirit. The church is to be the visible and living reality of the Holy of Holies on the Earth.[279] The church is supposed to be the visible manifestation of all the glory and majesty of the unseen throne room. The church is the body of Christ, the fullness of Him who fills all things.[280] It is the present manifestation of the Kingdom of God and the place that God has anointed to reveal the fullness of Christ Jesus, His only begotten Son.[281] The church as the manifestation of Jesus on the earth is fundamental to the New Covenant.[282] As the assembly of the Living God we are joined together with the heavenly Zion, the city of the living God, the heavenly Jerusalem.[283] God builds us up together as a holy habitation by the Holy Spirit even as one stone is laid upon another. Together, we appear as a holy temple in the Lord where acceptable sacrifices are offered to God.[284] Jesus Christ is the cornerstone of the holy church of God and we are those who are built together with Him as the holy habitation of the Almighty![285]

---

[279] (Eph 1:23; 5:32; 1 Cor 12:12, 27; Col 1:18; 2:9)
[280] (Eph 1:22-23)
[281] (Eph 4:11-13; 1 Cor 12:13; Mt 21:43; 1 Pet 2:9; Col 1:13)
[282] (Mt 6:18; 18:17; Ac 2:1, 47; 14:23; 20:28)
[283] (Heb 12:22-24, 10:25)
[284] (Eph 2:21-22)
[285] (1 Pet 2:6; Eph 2:22)

References

B. Lang, “כִּפֶּר,” in Theological Dictionary of the Old Testament, ed. G. Johannes Botterweck, Helmer Ringgren, and Heinz-Josef Fabry, trans. David E. Green (Grand Rapids, MI; Cambridge, U.K.: William B. Eerdmans Publishing Company, 1995), 290.

B. Lang, kipper, TDOT 7:289–90; L. Harris, (‘kpar’), (Theological Wordbook of the Old Testament)

Charles Simeon, Horae Homileticae: 2 Timothy to Hebrews, vol. 19 (London: Holdsworth and Ball, 1833), 215–216.

Charles Duke Yonge with Philo of Alexandria, The Works of Philo: Complete and Unabridged (Peabody, MA: Hendrickson, 1995), 561.

Friedrich Büchsel and Johannes Herrmann, “Ἵλεως, Ἱλάσκομαι, Ἱλασμός, Ἱλαστήριον,” in Theological Dictionary of the New Testament, ed. Gerhard Kittel, Geoffrey W. Bromiley, and Gerhard Friedrich (Grand Rapids, MI: Eerdmans, 1964–), 302.

George E. Mendenhall and Gary A. Herion, "Covenant," in The Anchor Yale Bible Dictionary, ed. David Noel Freedman (New York: Doubleday, 1992), 1179.

Jacob Milgrom, Leviticus 1–16: A New Translation with Introduction and Commentary, vol. 3, Anchor Yale Bible (New Haven; London: Yale University Press, 2008), 389.

Jacob Milgrom, A Continental Commentary: Leviticus: A Book of Ritual and Ethics (Minneapolis, MN: Fortress Press, 2004), 162.

Jacob Milgrom, "Atonement in the OT," IDBS, 78–82.

Marvin Richardson Vincent, Word Studies in the New Testament, vol. 3 (New York: Charles Scribner's Sons, 1887), 62.

Philo, Laws 1. 286, and the NOTE on "Fire came forth," 9:24)"

Robert Jamieson, A. R. Fausset, and David Brown, Commentary Critical and Explanatory on the Whole Bible, vol. 2 (Oak Harbor, WA: Logos Research Systems, Inc., 1997), 231.

The Anchor Bible Leviticus 1-16, Jacob Milgrom, Nov 1991.

Theological Dictionary of the New Testament, ed. Gerhard Kittel, Geoffrey W. Bromiley, and Gerhard Friedrich (Grand Rapids, MI: Eerdmans, 1964–), 255.

Thomas W. Mann, "Review of The Dethronement of Sabaoth. Studies in the Shem and Kabod Theologies, by Tryggve N. D. Mettinger," Journal of Biblical Literature 103 (1984): 268.

Bibles:

BHS (Biblical Hebraica Stuttgartensia- Hebrew Text), (2006)

Greek Byzantine Textform, (2005)

King James Version, (1900)

Jewish Publication Society (Masoretic Text), (1917)

Scrivener's Textus Receptus (1894)

Translation from Oldest Tradition, (2020)

Lexicons:

BDAG (A Greek-English lexicon of the New Testament and other early Christian Literature / revised and edited by Frederick William Danker.—3rd. ed.)

Enhanced Brown-Driver-Briggs Hebrew and English Lexicon, (1977).

Gesenius' Hebrew and Chaldee Lexicon to the Old Testament Scriptures, (2003)

Greek-English lexicon of the New Testament: Johannes P. Louw and Eugene Albert Nida, Greek-English Lexicon of the New Testament: Based on Semantic Domains (New York: United Bible Societies, (1996)

Lexham Research Lexicon of the Greek New Testament, Lexham Research Lexicons, (2020).

LSJ (A Greek-English lexicon Henry George Liddell et al., A Greek-English Lexicon), (1996)

About the Author

Dr. Mark Spitsbergen is the Senior Pastor of the Abiding Place in San Diego, California where he and his wife Anne have pastored since 1985. He holds a Bachelor of Arts Degree (BA) in Biology/Chemistry from Point Loma Nazarene University, a Master of Science (MS) from the University of Saint Andrews, a Doctorate of Theology (ThD) from School of Bible Theology, as well as a Doctorate of Ministry (D. Min.) from Life Christian University. He has been studying Biblical languages since 1983. He began his study of biblical languages at PLNU and also studied at UCSD with Dr. David Noel Freedman.

www.ingramcontent.com/pod-product-compliance
Lightning Source LLC
LaVergne TN
LVHW010612110826
845149LV00003B/874

* 9 7 9 8 9 9 4 4 0 9 8 7 9 *